ISBN: 978-0-9828378-8-7

The Best Jobs in the Film Industry

FILMMAKING

A Collaborative Art Form

Appreciations

A very special thank you to my children Tyler, Grace, Julia, Jayme, and Hayes who fill my life with love, joy, relevance, and sometimes confusion.

Thank you to my daughter Grace for helping to transcribe interviews, and rough editing this book as well as Sophie Paulette Jupillat for stepping in at the last moment to correct a mountain of grammatical errors.

Also, a big shout out and thank you to Jeff Matz, of Lure Design, Inc. located in Orlando, Florida for a simple yet elegant cover design. You truly are the best designer on the planet!

Last, but certainly not least, I thank God for the gift of life, breath, and my talents.

TABLE OF CONTENTS

Photo Courtesy of Jerry Enright

Introduction

If you've ever stayed to watch the credit roll of a feature film you are undoubtedly aware that there are sometimes 400 or more film crew working in every imaginable capacity. Unfortunately, I can't cover all of the jobs required to produce a large feature film because this book would be the size of the 'Lord of the Rings' trilogy and no one would even consider reading it.

The purpose of this book is simple; to give you, the aspiring filmmaker or crew member, a real life sampling of what some of the crew do on a daily basis - the good, bad and the ugly!

The Best Jobs in the Film Industry is largely written by the people who make feature films, but I hope those of you that are interested in tv production, gaming, marketing, industrial, corporate, advertising, indie films and other types of visual media will benefit from the job overviews and advice given by leaders in the field.

Making movies has not fundamentally changed in over 80 years, however the technology used to create and present them has advanced significantly. For those of you that aren't familiar with the basic filmmaking process there are many fine books that are dedicated to the process. I would encourage you to read several of them for an in-depth understanding of the industry; knowledge is power!

It is truly an exciting time to be in the film industry and it's growing exponentially on so many levels. Even my 17-year-old daughter Grace has approached me with script in hand, and has asked to borrow my HD camera so she and a friend could produce a film. This has happened so many times in fact that I finally gave her my camera! The funny thing is that now she can shoot on her iPhone X and produce an image that would have required a $300,000 camera just a few short years ago.

To keep my promise of making this a quick read I've gone back and deleted almost 80% of my personal commentary during the final edit to focus more on the industry professionals. My hope is that you will enjoy meeting some of the world's top filmmakers. Happy reading!

Contributors

One of the things I found most interesting while conducting my research is how the music and film industries are so different. In my last book, *The Best Jobs in the Music Industry* we explored music producers, recording engineers, and publishers and you would think that music and film, both being creative fields would share similarities, but in fact they don't.

Music is much more of a singular artistic pursuit, whereas filmmaking is a team sport. In the film world, all players come together in a team, expending enormous amounts of creative energy and sometimes money, in most cases to create a single 2-hour visual performance of which music is only a small part.

For the writing of this book, I had to become adept at developing relationships with the right people; something you will certainly need to learn if you haven't started already. The people I've interviewed for this book have been hand picked for who they are and the work they have done; it is a foregone conclusion that they know what they are talking about!

I am extremely grateful to everyone that has contributed to this book as they are among the elite in the film industry and in most cases 'Untouchable'. They have all graciously given their time to help you understand a little more about what they do for a living and the film business in general.

Overview

Working in the film industry can be rewarding on many levels, including creativity, individual expression, financial independence, and social interactivity, but is such a path right for you?

As sexy as the film business can be, it's not quite as glamorous as you might think. Although dazzling, a career in the film industry requires hard work, with incredibly long, unpredictable hours, accompanied by financial uncertainty. I would recommend you start your personal thought process by considering the basic benefits and challenges that you'll be presented with along the way and then decide if you really, really want to pursue a film career.

Benefits

For many on the film crew, working in a highly creative environment with coworkers that are pushing the envelope of 'what's possible,' is the single greatest reward and well worth the demanding work commitment. For the Visual Effects artist, it may be the opportunity to *paint* worlds that don't exist and work with high tech software that's not available to the general public. For the gaffer it may be the rewarding experience of *painting* with light.

It's fun to be part of a crew and participate in the creation of a film or tv show and it's no secret that walking around a closed set and interacting with actors and actresses is exciting.

Depending on how far you make it up the food chain, working in film can also be financially rewarding. Most crewmembers belong to a union and work hourly, or are contracted by the week, but some people with extensive experience or who have management positions negotiate a very good living.

In a few positions such as a successful director, composer, or producer they may negotiate other financial incentives, which include *points* (percentages of revenue), or *royalties*, which can be significant. In these cases, how much you might make depends on the financial success of the film itself.

Personally, I have always enjoyed the travel that can be associated with the making of a movie. It's fun to visit new places you could never afford to travel to, and today more than ever the production part of filmmaking has taken flight to destinations far from Hollywood. The reason for this is pretty simple … money. It is now much cheaper to film in a state that offers financial incentives usually in the form of tax refunds or paying the production company to hire local crew; these incentives can easily run into multi-million dollar production savings.

Challenges

So far, everything sounds pretty good - so what's the downside of working in film production? Let's start with the fact that you might frequently be unemployed, especially at the beginning of your career. A sustainable career in film requires you to have a well-honed skill set and a knack for meeting people.

Most of your jobs will come from referrals of other crew that enjoy working with you. Remember that while you are working, you won't be marketing yourself, so your next job is never guaranteed.

Another downside is time spent away from your family. If you're single, this isn't much of an issue, but missing your children's birthdays, or your fifth wedding anniversary are certainly not desirable. As I mentioned earlier, most films are not shot in Los Angeles, so that makes travel a necessity and depending on your family situation, it will be a challenge.

Next, the film needs to be completed and there is never enough money for overruns or a tolerance for those who want to work bankers' hours and get home in time for dinner. You may find yourself required to be up all night, prepping or shooting, only running on a few hours of sleep from the night before. There will be no mercy for you if you don't show up or fail to perform at the highest level. You'll just get fired and replaced immediately by one of the 1000 people waiting in line for you to fail, so they might have a chance to take your job!

Finally, I would say that *stress* is possibly the biggest issue I hear about from people in the business. If you were to combine financial insecurity with family pressures and long hours, it all adds up to stress, both emotional and physical. Some people thrive on it while others don't. You'll need to decide for yourself.

The Film Crew

'Film crew', or just 'crew' is the term given to the people involved in the technical or practical aspects of shooting a film and are typically hired by a production company that is in turn hired by a studio or group of investors (partners). Unlike the cast, they are considered to be behind the camera.

Working on a film production is exhilarating, but there can be incredible pressure to solve impossible problems on a continual basis. People that are successful in the film industry have well developed interpersonal skills as well as identifiable traits. As you look at this list below you might be saying to yourself, "Of course I have all of those ", and in fact you would be lucky if you do, but I can tell you from my own experience that only a minuscule segment of the population does.

Some of the traits of a successful film production film crew are:

- *Responsible* - to others and the production (someone to be depended upon)
- *Willingness* - to jump in and help others. (Every time)
- *Problem Solver* - this business is about problems and those that know how to fix them.
- *Sense of Humor* - the ability to see the world through a filter of humor and not take yourself too seriously.
- *Dedication* - to the art, to the craft, to the project, and to your fellow crewmembers.
- *Always learning* - just as in life, staying on top of the job's continual evolution.
- *Dependability* - being on time is invaluable to the crew because all areas of the filmmaking are interdependent.
- *Creative* - in every aspect of the business! This is a business of creativity; that's why everyone wants to be in it.
- *Competency* – being the best at what you do and never compromising.

Generally speaking, film crew jobs can be categorized into one of the following areas:

Producers and Director - Funding, legal, distribution, vision and management

Creative - Screenplay and associated vision presentation

Production Design - Overall physical look of the film

Art Direction - Supervise, manage and bring unity to the directors vision

Hair, Make-up, and Wardrobe – Working with talent

Camera - Shoots the film

Lighting and Electrical - Lighting the set and all wiring

Production Sound - Captures the sound during production

Visual Effects - Practical digital effects creation

Sound Edit & Design - Dialogue editing and sound effect creation

Film Edit – Cutting the film together under the direction of the director

Music - Composing and licensing of all music

Production Assistants - Work with and for everybody

Marketing – Promotion of the film through various sources

The above list just includes the main job categories. There are numerous other jobs associated with each heading

THE FIVE PHASES OF FILMMAKING

The making of a film is generally thought of as happening in three phases, but there are actually five (with additional sub-categories). Most jobs associated with movie making fall into one of the following phases: Development, Preproduction, Production, Postproduction, and Distribution.

Development: The idea is found (or created/written/adapted). It's at this early stage that you will think about the process, funding, characters, research, and look and feel of a film. It also becomes a decision point - move forward, or stop.

Preproduction is the process of pulling all of the key elements of a film together including financing (which is a process onto itself), the screenplay, selection of the director and cinematographer, principle cast, crew, etc.

Production is the actual process of creating the content (shooting the film) including principle photography and so on.

Postproduction: When all of the visual content is edited, special effects are added, dialogue edited, music scored, sound sfx/foley added, and the final film is prepared for release and public viewing at your local theater, on Netflix, or wherever.

Distribution is the final phase of any production and relates to marketing, and delivery of the finished production.

More detail…

In its most basic form, the process of developing a feature film project works something like this:

Someone has an idea for a film and then needs to find the funds to produce it into a movie or tv series. This is called the *development* phase and requires a script, or screenplay, a producer, director, financial connections, principal casting, and a loose selection of proposed department heads.

PREPRODUCTION

Once all of these developmental tasks are in place the film is *'Green-lit'* and moves on to a phase called Preproduction where the director of Photography is hired, the script is 'locked' (sort of), design and construction of sets begins, the production schedule is agreed upon, locations chosen, and special effects are identified.

Related jobs:

Director, Screenwriter, producer, Storyboard Artist, Art Director, Location Manager/Scout, Casting Director, Production Designer, Costume Designer

PRODUCTION

The next phase of filmmaking is 'Production'. This is when all of the visual content is filmed and/or created in harmony with the animators and actors/actresses (talent), under the director. This is a monumental undertaking and also where the real *fun* begins. On larger productions there may be hundreds of crew involved.

Short list of production jobs:

Director, Cinematographer/Director of Photography, Camera operator, 1st Assistant Director, Production Manager, Makeup, SFX, Gaffer, Grip, Best Boy, Production sound, Boom operator, Production Assistant, Script Supervisor, Transportation, Accounting, Stunts, Grip, Set Dresser, Key Scenic, Prop Maker, Prop Master.

POSTPRODUCTION

The last major phase of feature filmmaking is called Postproduction, or 'Post' for short. The production crew is now on to its next adventure and the postproduction supervisor, film editor, music composer, special effects, animation, and sound crews are fully engaged working with the producers, and Director to complete the envisioned masterpiece. Postproduction usually takes much more time than the actual shooting of the film and it's not unusual for a feature film to spend over a year in post.

During postproduction there are also many other important business functions running concurrently in the background including marketing, accounting, and distribution. This is when many important questions are addressed; 'Where will our masterpiece play and for how long, what can we expect in terms of 'Long-Tail' revenue (money made over time) from foreign distribution, cable, DVD, soundtracks, iTunes, Netflix and other media outlets?'

While the production crew is busy making the movie there are numerous people working to leverage the film and make as much money as possible for the investors who have funded the project. Investors in the film business are not easy to come by and expect a reasonable ROI (Return on investment).

Short list of postproduction jobs (there are hundreds):

Film Editor, Music Editor, Dialogue Editor, Composer, Orchestrator, Animators, Re-Recording Mixer, Colorist

* * *

Like most people, I find the film business fascinating. There's nothing like walking outside at night and seeing the sun shining brightly. That's exactly what happened when I came out of my downtown plaza office in Santa Fe, New Mexico one night and they were shooting inserts for the film '*Odd Thomas*'. Huge squares of lights hung from cranes that overhung the entire square literally turning night into day.

Finding your way in the film industry will surely be a wild journey and there are thousands of bloodied bodies lining the road to Hollywood. Competition even for the very talented is tough, and relationships are more important than most any other business.

On the upside, there are more films being made today than at any other time in history and not just in the USA. Consider that India is churning out over 900 films a year! Features sometimes employ hundreds of crew and the jobs range from director to construction workers, to accountants and legal teams, not to mention the marketing people that promote the films.

EXECUTIVE PRODUCER

Executive producers (EP) are key to a film because they are typically responsible for either funding, or arranging the funding. Without them, a film can't get off the ground. Of course, the EP is also involved in many other ways, like making sure the production is running on schedule and that the story remains engaging so that the finished project will be marketable.

I spoke with a couple of Hollywood's top executive producers and learned that there is much more to this job than I ever imagined.

Steven Saxton, Chairman, Founder and CEO of Hollywood Studios has had a long successful career in the film business. He was most recently one of the executive producer's for the feature film *Lone Survivor* where his main responsibility was funding and distribution.

Steven Saxton (right) with Mark Ruffalo

STEVEN SAXTON

Executive Producer

IMDB - Lone Survivor, The Kids are All Right, The Life and Death of John Gotti

Q: Steven, it's a pleasure to ask you a few questions and I'd like to start with a basic one. As the Executive Producer of a film like *Lone Survivor,* what do you do?

A: A couple of our films, *2 Guns* and *Lone Survivor* mostly shared the same team. My relationship was with the foreign distributor, producers and the financier's of both pictures.

My main responsibility was to arrange and supply the critical equity (money) needed to finance the pictures. Both of these films were in production and weeks into principal photography while the bond companies were all scrambling to close the principle photography loan. The films were both in severe jeopardy of shutting down at this critical time, so I keep the train moving forward…that's what I do.

Q: Is the EP expected to find funding for a picture?

A: Sometimes yes. The executive producer usually brings the major elements of a project together including: financing, domestic distribution, foreign distribution, the script, the director or a major star.

Many times The EP also might be managing the director, writer or star of the project.

Q: I have been told that in many cases 'Producer' is simply a title and is not attached to any tangible responsibility. Are there different types of 'Producer' roles that have different responsibilities, or is it a negotiated credit of some kind?

A: There are executive producers, producers and line producers. The contracts of the 'producers' always have negotiated terms. Typically the 'producer' has had something significant to do with the script, development process, writer, attaching the director or talent (packaging), distribution, or financing.

The 'line producer' is the physical on-set 'producer' and in charge of the day-to-today production.

Q: Given that there is no 'typical day', would you tell me about yours?

A: Structuring financing for a film, (i.e., closing a loan against foreign pre-sales, tax incentives, gap financing, and closing equity). I might also be working out complications with the budget or conflicts with distributors (studios), directors, talent, producers, managers, lawyers, agents and financiers (Millionaires & Billionaires). My days are busy!

Q: Tell me something that most people don't know about you, Steven?

A: I love movies, especially the really good ones and have enormous respect for all of those whom contribute to the process of filmmaking. I have had the honor of being knighted by The Sovereign Order of St. John of Jerusalem Knights of Malta, Catholic Copts; nominated by Prince Don Antonio Ruspoli and approved by Cardinal Stephanos II, Ghattas, Patriarch of Alexandria and blessed by Pope John Paul II.

Q: What was the craziest thing you've ever experienced on a film project?

A: *The Kids Are Alright* was an exciting journey. I was involved in the early stages of the project (no pre-sales, no domestic distribution in place) and the film was in Preproduction but the financing was still not closed.

We took the film to the Sundance Film Festival and screened it to a full theater of distributors and watched as the hype turned into a major bidding war, with the film ultimately being sold that same evening at a party to Focus Features.

Rumor had it, if the theater had burned down, the entire independent film distribution industry would have been wiped out, as everyone in the business was in attendance. That film was nominated for 62 awards and won 13 of them including a Golden Globe for best picture and best actress (Annette Bening). It was quite an exciting ride!

Q: What role if any, has formal education played in what you do today?

A: 'Education and Knowledge are Power', it's an on-going process and I continue to learn something new everyday.

Q: What is the most challenging part of your role as Executive producer?

A: Keeping all of the balls up in the air including the script, writers, star, director, distribution, agents, managers, lawyers, financiers, major egos and multiple conflicting opinions.

Q: How is the executive producer typically compensated?

A: Typically it's a fee with back-end participation, and On-Screen credits.

Q: Is there a logical career path that leads someone to the position of EP?

A: Maybe having a father that is #3 in Forbes like Megan Ellison wouldn't hurt!

Q: Are you involved in the actual production of a film (on set)?

A: Yes. My company has acted as managers to writers, director and talent. Other times we are the financiers, producers and foreign distributors.

Q: Do you have any advice for a young person that wants to enter the business side of the film industry?

A: Try to establish as many relationships as you can with successful people in the industry because knowledge and relationships are the key that will open the door to 'OZ'. These are the people you can learn from and hopefully collaborate with down the road.

Q: Steven, have you ever had an intern, or mentored someone?

A: Through the years my companies have always worked with interns. Some have gone on to become executives at my companies; while others moved on to have extremely successful careers in Hollywood.

Q: Any other wisdom you might like to pass along?

A: This one of the most difficult and sought after businesses in the world. It can also be one of the most rewarding. Remember to stay focused on your goal, be calm, breathe and enjoy the ride.

Another very busy Executive Producer Mark Kamine added his thoughts to the position. Early on in his career, Mark worked his as a location manager and now acts as both a unit production manager and executive producer depending on the film project.

MARK KAMINE

Executive Producer

IMDB - Silver Linings Playbook, Shutter Island, American Hustle, Ted, God's Pocket

Q: What is the difference between the role of 'producer' and the 'Executive producer'?

A: Producers usually originate the project in some way - whether by commissioning or buying the script, buying rights to a book or a remake, etc. On indie films like *God's Pocket*, the executive producer is probably raising the funds if not partially supplying them personally.

These days' executive producers can come from a lot of places. It's often a credit given to line producers but you'll also see this credit given to actors' managers, studio people (who might never show up on set), investors, and lots of other people getting that credit (or the co-producer credit) as well.

Q: So if I understand correctly, many times, a person with the title of Executive producer may not have any actual responsibility to the film in terms of creativity, final product, distribution etc.?

A: There are sometimes producers (not just EPs) that are credited on films who have no input beyond the check they wrote or the fact that they're someone's brother or sister. Producers might be managers, mothers, fathers, girlfriends or boyfriends. These people are very important to the actors no doubt and may have encouraged the actor to do the film but have little or nothing to do with the film itself. I'm sure there are many stranger reasons than these for the bestowal of producer credits.

Q: Is the executive producer expected to find funding for a picture?

A: It depends. Pretty much any 'producer' credit can be a person who finds funding, but there's no particular expectation. It depends on the reason that person is there. In the case of *God's Pocket*, the people who found the funding are called 'Producers', no modifier, along with a few other key people - Philip Seymour Hoffman and his producing partner. They were the prime reason the movie got made - they took John Slattery's script, which he co-wrote with the idea of directing, and helped him get the actors. They commissioned line producer Erika Hampson to create a budget and schedule, which they then presented to the people with the money, who decided I guess that it was worth financing at the given price. On *American Hustle*, two of the executive producers came with David O. Russell from *Silver Linings* and were there for him, while one of the EP's was from the originating studio (Annapurna) and was assigned to the film to keep track of things with their interests in mind.

Q: Tell me about what might you be doing during production to move a film in the right direction.

A: In prep, I'm usually trying to keep tabs on everything – are the sets getting built on time, are we locking (choosing) locations that are acceptably priced and located, is the crew hired is the equipment ordered.

During production I have tended to mostly hang around the set so people can find me with production questions, e.g., can they have extra help the next day, can they order another camera or add more crew for big days, can I help them find a replacement for someone who isn't working out. I'll also keep an eye on how the day is going – are we getting the work done, and if not why not, and is there anything to be done about it.

Sometimes you go slower than you originally planned and you just have to live with it; sometimes you go faster and you try to think what else you can do. On set the 1st assistant director is running things – it's usually their schedule you end up working off of and that person is the best source of information as to how things are going and if not well, why.

Q: **Tell me something that most people don't know about you.**

A: I was an English Major in college and did some freelance writing and editing before going to film school and starting my work on movies. I also read a lot and for a the last twelve years have written book reviews for the 'Times Literary Supplement' (London), and 'New York Times' as well as a number of other places. So when I'm buried in my computer I'm not always looking at the budget!

Q: **What was the best time you've ever had working on a film and why?**

A: Well *The Fighter* was a great project because we pretty much all stayed in the same roadside Marriott outside Lowell, MA, where most of the film was shot. David O. Russell, Amy Adams, Melissa Leo, and just about every actor who came and went stayed there while Wahlberg had an apartment not far away. It was a very tight group of people, with some nice weekend barbecues not to mention a great script.

It's also interesting to enter a different world (in that case the world of boxing) and hang out with people like Micky Ward and Dick Ecklund and the trainers and fighters from the local gym. Overall it was a very nice experience, and the fact that it was great film enhances the memory.

Q: **What is the most challenging part of your job?**

A: The toughest part of producing at my level, where I'm mostly trying to keep things more or less on schedule and budget, is to balance the purely financial side with the creative side. Sometimes you have to let things go long or over budget to make a better movie and you hope to make it up somewhere down the road.

Q: How is the Executive Producer compensated?

A: It's usually a weekly fee, or an overall fee for the project broken up between prep, shoot and post, where you get 20% during prep, 60% during shooting, 10% during Postproduction and 10% on delivery of the film. Unfortunately, executive producers don't normally get percentages of the profits and box office bonuses; these are reserved for the producers, actors, and the director.

PRODUCER

In days past, the credit roll on a film or tv show included a producer or two. These days you might see 20 or more. I found this pretty confusing until producer Olivier Arnesen broke it down for me.

Olivier and I worked together for several years at my production company RedHouse. We was in charge of all production and made sure we stayed on budget, could find talent in Spain that spoke Catalan, the perfect location for every shot, even the best seats on our flights. Olivier greatly contributed to our success while consistently bringing a high level of professionalism, and fun into the mix.

OLIVIER ARNESEN

Producer

IMDB – Pirates of the Caribbean, Body of Lies, National Treasure, Ballers

Q: Olivier, I'm so happy to talk to you. In short what does a Producer do?

A: The role of producer varies depending on the type of production. For example the news producer, commercial producer, episodic/tv producer and film producer all have vastly different roles and responsibilities.

With respect to what I do in episodic tv, the following applies to people with a producer credit: Commonly, the UPM (unit production manager) of record will also be given a producer and/or executive producer title. This person oversees the overall budgeting of a tv series, hires all the department heads and interfaces with the studio (example HBO) with respect to the budget, cast, *and* creative.

Other individuals with the producer title, co-producer title, or associate producer title will have varying responsibilities that may include the following:

1. They are part of the production management team that works directly for and under the EP/UPM managing the set up and operations of a production office, stages, warehouse etc. They will also hire crew, manage all equipment rentals i.e. camera, grip, electric and specialty equipment like techno, cranes, drones, leasing of boats, jets, etc.
2. They could also be someone whose responsibility it is to deal with stunt casting/cameos of real people and managing production placement deals.
3. The individual who oversees all of postproduction might be given a producer credit.
4. They may also be a writer on the series where they get either a producer and/or executive producer credit.

So, as you can see it varies and is usually up to the show runner/creator and studio to give out these titles.

Q: How would I become a Producer?

A: In the traditional sense of episodic tv and/or film and but not news or commercials someone who wants to become a producer will typically follow the route of landing a job as a production assistant in the production office, then moving their way through the ranks to becoming a production secretary, assistant production coordinator, production coordinator, production supervisor, upm and finally producer.

This path is really all considered production management. If you are an idea person and creator of sorts and can pitch a great story for either tv or a film that's another path.

Q: Working on a show like *Ballers*, what specifically are your responsibilities?

A: My job responsibility includes setting up the working infrastructure for offices, stages, warehouses and storage. Generally, productions start from scratch so I handle all equipment including camera, grip, electric and specialty equipment (cranes, planes, helicopters, boats, etc.)

I also interface with the department heads for the above and others with respect to what is budgeted for rentals. I participate in the handling of insurance has it relates to all rentals as well.

In addition I work with the AD department and help facilitate bringing in technical advisers that specialize in military operations, police offices, doctors etc. that may be outside their scope of responsibility.

Q: Are you part of a union?

A: Yes, I am part of Local IATSE 161. The majority of the crew is union, including actors with the exception of above the line personnel.

Q: Best advice you have for someone entering the film industry?

A: Do the research, find a career coach, decide what you want to do and stick with it because focus and continuity pays off!

Q: Do you mentor or have interns on your shows?

A: I mentor all the time. I do so with the PA's we have on staff.

Q: How do producers like yourself physically get paid?

A: Like all crew, I get paid through a payroll company like 'Cast & Crew' or

'Entertainment Partners'. All episodic tv shows and/or films use one of these 2 payroll companies. There are smaller ones but these two are widely used.

SCREENWRITER

This next job may be out of order, but let's look at one scenario …

Once we have successfully pitched a concept for a movie and have funding (even if partial) we are at the point where we can start to seriously talk about making a film. We won't address how many films never make it this far, or crash and burn during this process but I can assure that it's in the 95-percentile range.

As I said mentioned earlier, it all starts with an idea so lets introduce you to a screenwriter. Sometimes the idea starts with the screenwriter and other times they are hired on as writing contractors. This is a very cool job that is both rewarding and extremely challenging due to the large number of stakeholders with their own *ideas* that must be appeased during the writing process. Remember that old saying, 'Everyone has an opinion' and 'Ideas are a dime a dozen'? Well, they take on new meaning in the film world. If you were the one putting up the money to fund a film, you would expect your ideas to be taken seriously even if they weren't any good!

Finding a notable writer was quite a challenge, so I was pleasantly surprised when a good friend and amazing music supervisor, Greg Sill made an introduction to Graham, a renowned screenwriter that on my own I would never have been able to reach. Graham is quietly brilliant, never boastful (even though he has good reason to be), informative, and generous with his time. We talked casually about the business, his upbringing, and a few things every aspiring screenwriter should know.

Graham Yost

Screenwriter

IMDB - Speed, The Pacific, Band of Brothers, Justified, The Americans

Q: Graham, what influence did your education have on your career choice?

A: Well, I really valued my education at Trinity College and the University of Toronto but there is this modern view of a university college education that it should be career driven and focused on the future and making money. That's not at all what education was about when I was growing up. I still wish that I could go back to school with a little more interest and drive because I felt like most of my studies were just taking time away from girls and pinball and football!

Q: So, if college didn't prepare you for that you do today, would you explain how you ended up in the film industry?

A: My father had a television show in Toronto for 25 years, so my brother and I grew up in a house where we talked about movies and books all the time. Later I applied to the master's film program at Columbia and didn't get in so I took a summer film course at NYU. It was a great course and we made six short films in six weeks.

I then decided to stay in New York. I had a friend who had graduated from the Columbia journalism school and one day we looked at the job board and there were opportunities to write for the Encyclopedia Britannica and the Soap Opera Digest so I jumped on it.

In my off hours I worked on an idea that I'd been tossing around prior to the move and while I knew that the first draft wasn't very good I knew that the idea was. So, I kept rewriting that script and it turned out to be a big turning point for me. Instead of just abandoning that script and going onto the next one I really worked at making something better, which I ultimately did.

Q: Did you plan on being a writer who specialized in dialogue, action, or romance?

A: That's a good question. I think that some people do become branded. It's interesting because when *Justified* was running I'd be approached for modern westerns by feature producers, but when I was starting out I would say that I was trying to write comedy and really good action films.

Q: Pivotal moments in your career?

A: I've been very lucky along the way. One day you get a call from your agent and she says, "Tom Hanks wants to do a miniseries at HBO about the Apollo space program, are you interested?"

And I said, "I'm in."

Working on *Band of Brothers*, *From the Earth to the Moon*, and *The Pacific,* changed my life and now I frequently get calls about doing mini-series. I also receive regular pitches for action films, because of *'Speed'*, and going the distance with *Justified* has given me a degree of credibility in the commercial television series world.

Q: I've been told that you are a terrific showrunner. It's a complex job that I purposely left out of this book but might you give us an overview?

A: Sure. First of all it is a very peculiar job. I keep on trying to find parallels with the rest of the world, and the closest I can come to is a football coach, in that you're at the head of this big organization working for the owner.

The showrunner has to deal with a wide array of different personalities, which includes the actors, the writers, and the crew. A lot of this job is about whom you hire; you have to make a lot of choices like who's going to be your offensive coordinator, your defensive coordinator, your special team, who is being cast, who are the directors you're going to be working with and in the case of *Justified*, who is on your writing staff?

The thing that was fantastic about *Justified* was working with seasoned professionals like producers, Sarah Timberman and Carl Beverly, and Michael Dinner who was our directing producer. Michael would hire all the directors while Sarah and Carl handled most of the interactions with the network and the studio and all the financial stuff. Then on top of that I had a writer's room with one of *those* staffs, just amazing people!

So, ultimately for a showrunner it's your responsibility to be producing and delivering scripts, everything else is important, but everything else can be delegated. Making sure the scripts are coming out on time is your number one priority.

Q: As a writer, are you writing for the 'blue sky' version of your idea, or are you trying to place your creativity relative to the production budget?

A: The biggest change for production in the past 20 years has been computer-generated imagery (CGI). You can do just about anything now; you can make any movie, any story, or any shot, and, for a much more reasonable budget than one could imagine. You can do things in a television show now that they couldn't afford to do in movies 30 years ago. That said, your first responsibility when writing a script is to write the best possible story.

Now, when you're writing a television pilot you have to keep in mind that the budget is going to be this, the number of shooting days is going to be that. You can't have Genghis Kahn and the Mongol hordes, overrunning Samarkhand, but maybe you could do it for *Game of Thrones*.

Although, what I love about *Game of Thrones* is the first couple seasons you get to the battle and… the battle is coming… the battle's coming… and then it cuts to: it's the day after the battle! Even for HBO's budget, battles are expensive. So, you want to keep it in mind, and in line.

I can give you a concrete example of what you might write for television. Three years ago one of the writers on *Justified*, Taylor Elmore, one of the best writers I've ever worked with, came up with a show called *The Wild Blue*, about life on an aircraft carrier. He just wrote it, and there were takeoffs and tail hooks and flight deck, below deck, hangars, helicopters flying in, and it was just "okay, how can we do it"? Can we get the help from the Navy? If we can't, what do we green screen? What can we build? As you can see, it just became another problem for us to solve. The show didn't go forward for many other reasons, but that was going to be a show set on an aircraft carrier, and an absolutely monstrous problem to pull off, but it was still in the realm of possibility.

Q: Graham, have you ever wanted to direct?

A: Not really, I mean, there's always an urge to try directing and I think that pretty much everyone in this business is interested in sitting in that chair. People have asked me over the years, why I didn't or was I going to direct any of the *Justified* episodes. The practical reality is being a showrunner is there's no time to direct, unless you're going to direct the last episode. And, when we have directors like Michael Dinner and Adam Arkin, it's like; I'm not going to do a better job than that.

So as a showrunner I don't feel the need to direct. However, on *Earth to the Moon*, and then on *Pacific*, I thought that I would take a shot if they would let me. On *Earth to the Moon*, I got my chance and it was probably the best time I ever had in the business. Just a blast, because I was working with friends and a great crew; it was just so much fun. It was also a story I was in love with.

Q: Would you talk a little about how writers are paid, Graham?

A: Well, first off we have a fantastic Guild and the Guild sets minimums, so there's a certain amount you're going to be paid for a teleplay, for an hour of television or a half hour of television. There have been divisions over the years between network and cable, and cable gets less. We're trying to change that so there's more parity and because television has changed so radically. I mean, what is television now? If it includes Amazon, and Hulu, and Netflix, it's just a shorter, smaller screen, I guess.

In some cases you can get paid by the episode and features have minimums, but very few people ever just get the minimum. Similarly, in a television show where I get my money, and most writers make their money it's not what they're paid for the script but whether or not they're on the writing staff for that show.

On any tv show, you'll see so many producer credits run before the show, - well that's because most of those people are writers. If you see consulting producer, supervising producer, co-executive producer, and executive producer, most of those people are writers and they get paid a producing fee on top of their writing fee.

Q: So, what is the hierarchy of the writing staff?

A: It's a rough pyramid, in that the showrunner is at the top and then you'll have a number two, and he or she is responsible for running the room when you're not around. Then you'll have a number three and a number four, and they're responsible for running the room when the number two isn't there. And it sort of goes down like that. It goes predominantly by the credits, and the credits go predominantly by seniority so if you were the story editor on one show, you might be executive script producer on the next, and then move up to co-producer and then executive. I may have that wrong somewhere in there but that's the basic hierarchy

Q: Tell me about some of the bad stuff you've had to deal with?

A: The reality is when "bad stuff" happens, like you lose a location, you're running out of light, all this stuff; well that's a great problem. Come on - you're making a television show. You're working in movies! You get to do this and figure it out! To me that's the fun part.

I remember the last day we had Tim Olyphant on the set of *Justified* and he was flying off that afternoon, to Munich to work on Oliver Stone's Snowden film. We had to get him out at a certain time, and we're looking at what we had scheduled for the day, so I said, "We've got to cut that scene" to Sarah Timberman and she said, "Well, what if that scene in front of the house actually took place in the park, and we combined and made it all one thing."

I said, "Great idea," and she went off and wrote a draft of the scene and sent it back to me, and we solved the problem and it ended up being a great scene. That's the fun of it, solving the problem. Come on, I'm a kid that grew up in Toronto, and the fact that I even get to do this makes me the luckiest guy. Your series is called Best Jobs, right? I'm one of the guys who have got the best job. I love that I get to do this!

Q: What's your best advice for a young person starting out that wants your job?

A: One of the best parts of being a writer is that we can always write. A director needs actors to act and a crew to direct. Actors need something to perform. Writers can always write. So my best advice is to always be writing.

DIRECTOR

At this point we have a script and hopefully some money. This is when the machine gains momentum and the crew starts to come together.

Film crews vary by size and depending on the level (budget) of production, can have as many as 3000+ people on a single crew like *Iron Man 3* which set a record with 3310 crew members *(reference IMDB)*

Let's talk about the director. They are much like a concertmaster; the person with a vision and the entire crew is devoted to delivering their vision. Directors come in many forms in the film industry, and even though this book focuses on feature films, I believe there is a lot to learn from directors working outside Hollywood.

I've had the pleasure of working with advertising, feature film, and documentary directors. I've even directed a few short films myself, which has given me a large measure of respect for those that direct for a living. Being a film director requires a magical mix of skills that include: creativity, authority, grace under fire, communication skills, problem solving, decisiveness, vision and most importantly a good mind for detail

Thousands of documentaries are released each year but only one director receives an Oscar for 'Director of Best Documentary Feature'. A couple of years ago, it was Morgan Neville that walked to the stage to accept the Oscar. Morgan is well known for his documentary work in the music industry, and has a special way of making you comfortable when he's talking to you. I enjoyed speaking with Morgan very much.

Morgan Neville (Top Right) interviewing Keith Richards

MORGAN NEVILLE

Director

IMDB -Twenty Feet from Stardom, Johnny Cash's America, Keith Richards, Abstract: The Art of Design

Q: Morgan, would you tell my readers about your path into filmmaking?

A: Growing up I always had a few main passions, music, movies and writing. I thought that music and movies were kind of hobbies and writing was a career because journalism seemed like a real career, which was what I was interested in. When I attended the University of Pennsylvania I wrote for the college paper and loved journalism, but I was missing music and movies.

So, I decided to make my first film, which was a historical documentary about my hometown of Los Angeles. I wanted to document how Angelinos saw their city, their own history, and how different it was. I remember starting this project and within two weeks calling my parents and saying " This is what I'm going to do with the rest of my life." It was just a perfect fit and I knew it instantly, because documentary filmmaking is filming and journalism combined. I describe it as 3D journalism.

Q: What are some of the differences between making a feature film and a Documentary?

A: I would say documentary filmmaking has at least as much to do with journalism as it does to do with filmmaking. Another difference is that I think documentaries are like backwards films.

In other words if you're making a Hollywood movie you first write a script, and then shoot a movie. If you're making a documentary you shoot a movie, then write a script. Documentary filmmaking is also a process of exploration; people ask what's the #1 skill you need to be a documentarian and I always say 'curiosity'. I love to learn, and for somebody who loves to learn there is no better job.

Q: So: you're making backwards films, and sometimes you don't know exactly where they might take you. Have you ever been deep into a project and then thought, "This is not going where I need it to go"

A: Well sure, that happens... often.

Making a film, even like *20 Feet from Stardom* is a perfect example because I loved the characters but there was no story when I started. Nobody had ever even written a book about back ground singers. I interviewed a lot of singers from totally different backgrounds who sang for James Brown, or in Nashville, or girl groups and after about fifty interviews stood back to look at what the story might be.

In this case I said, "Well, there are about ten stories here." It could have gone in so many directions but I picked the first and biggest story of backup singing, which was kind of the revolution of black singers coming into the white music world and the various iterations of that sound over generations.

Even as we were editing the film it was a struggle to get the story together. I know a lot of filmmakers that have actually hit brick walls and they just weren't able to finish their films, which must be painful.

Q: Would you tell us about your close connection to music?

A: Well, after a few years of making documentary films I thought I'd try my hand at making a music film because it would allow me to use my love and knowledge of music to bring it. It didn't hurt that I was also a musician!

I think the best music films really allow their music to tell the story and that the music itself drives both the story and character. I mean, some of my favorite music documentaries are about bands I don't like but they are still very emotional and powerful. For example a band like Anvil (I don't own any Anvil albums) the songs work because they drive the character in that film. Or, a documentary film I just watched by Jason Becker, *Not Dead Yet*, about this metal guitarist who has Lou Gehrig's disease; he was diagnosed in his prime and now composes symphonies using nothing but his eyes.

I should mention that all of this leads to another thing, which is that the music can also be used simply as a vehicle to bring the audience in and allow you to tell other types of stories about civil rights, race, gender, love or whatever you like

Sometimes people ask me "Do you get sick of making music films" and I say "Well no, because they're all completely different. Do you get sick of listening to music, or sick of reading novels?"

There is just so much diversity in my work … I'm currently working on a film with Yo-Yo Ma. We're shooting in Jordan, and China; it's a totally different world from dealing with say, Memphis soul and STAX records. To me it's a great way of concurrently nourishing my love of music and my curiosity.

Q: Morgan, there are advantages and disadvantages to being the Writer and the tv on a film, could you talk about that?

A: I'd say that to me they are indivisible. In a documentary the script is part of the film making process and the editors are take on a bigger role than a DP. So, it's really collaboration between you (the director) and the editor.

I've written lots of scripts and the idea of having someone else write your films really undercuts the voice of the director. The greater challenge is being a producer and a director because you're trying to balance the creative with how much the production is going to cost and where you're going to get the next grant - that's the real struggle. It shouldn't be a surprise that documentary filmmaking is a hard world to make a living in.

Q: My next question is mostly directed towards the music you use in your films - how do you deal with all the licensing and copyright and original masters? I know it can be very political, and expensive.

A: I'd say films like *20 Feet from Stardom* are the hardest of films you can make from a music clearance point of view. My quick explanation is this: If you're making a film about a band or singer or a record label or something like that all the music tends to come from one source. You have a record label, music publisher, agent, manager or a band that has vested interest in seeing your film get made.

If you're making a film like *20 Feet from Stardom* or for that matter, Denny Tedesco's *The Wrecking Crew* you're sampling music from all over, from people that had no power, agents, or labels behind them and you're using big songs for people who played sometimes minor roles in them. It can be very hard to secure the rights because you've got to go everywhere to get the songs cleared.

Q: I have to ask you this, being a musician myself. Musicians as a group can be very temperamental, and as a tv doing a lot of interview type work, has attitude ever been an issue?

A: Not everybody is easy, and I've certainly had some hard interviews, but I'd say 99% of them turn out to be good interviews; I wouldn't say easy but I would say good.

Part of it is having interviewed hundreds if not thousands of people as a journalist, before I started making films. My skills as an interviewer are one of the strongest things I have going and I've been doing this for over twenty years.

An interview should be a conversation not an interrogation. What that means is simply to be curious, and listen. Ask follow-up questions and stay engaged; don't try and show off what you know. Also, go in very prepared; I write out questions, but then when I start interviews I never look at my questions.

Specifically for on-camera interviews, you've got to keep eye contact to be in the conversation. Even when I start shooting I don't want to say "Lights, camera, action", and I never ask them to repeat the answers.

Q: When somebody is looking at a career as a documentarian and filmmaker what might you tell them would be a good way to get started?

A: I would say the most practical way to start is to have a skill. You can break down all documentary jobs to one of three categories: production jobs, Postproduction jobs and producing jobs.

I would say that depending on their skills are they should pick one area and develop those skills so they have a way in. For instance, I'm always looking for a great editor, and even a great assistant editor is a good path. I've promoted many assistant editors who are now directing, particularly in documentary because it's such an editor's medium.

Q: **How has winning the Oscar for** *20 Feet from Stardom* **changed your personal vision or the type of projects you might be looking at for the future?**

A: It has. Fundraising has become easier. It's not *easy* but easier. A lot of people have come forward and said, "What do you want to do? I want to help you make whatever film you want to make." Other people also call me with projects they need help on - I get at least one call a day. I'm still the same filmmaker; I just think it's hopefully going to be easier from here on out to do what I want to do.

Like they say - it took you twenty years to become an overnight success!
Q: I have to ask you this one last thing because I am curious. Being a musician yourself, how does winning an Oscar compare to having head nods for Grammys.

A: Maybe I'm biased now but everything else pales.

Several years ago while running a production company in Orlando, Florida we were in need of a talented editor. My partner at the time, director Dan O'Loane recommended we interview Glenn Lazarro, a friend of his from NYC, who had been credited for creating the MTV editorial style. His amazing talent and ability to take someone's undeveloped ideas, spin his magic, and turn them into something very special through the editing process struck me immediately. Glenn has gone on to become one of the top commercial directors in the advertising world and currently runs *99 Tigers*, a very successful production company.

GLENN LAZZARO

Commercial Director

IMDB - TV, ESPN, Pepsi, Shear Genius, Step it up Dance

Q: Glenn, It's been a long time since we spoke and in that time you've become one of the most sought after Commercial Directors in NYC. Would you explain your thoughts on the differences between a Commercial Director and a feature film Director?

A: I don't make movies; I just watch and get inspiration from them. I think the big difference is whether you're better at telling a story in 30 seconds or in 2 hours. I've always liked the pace and intensity of that 30-second window.

Q: How do you decide which projects to take on at your production company 99 Tigers?

A: When tv networks and other clients come to us with work, we almost never say no. Whether it's a small, low-budget job or some huge project, we see opportunity in everything. Sometimes the small, invisible jobs let you be your most creative. But what we look for in most jobs are the ones that let us write, create, and really put our vision into it.

Q: What are the most important skills someone would need to be successful as a commercial director?

A: Some of the best directors start their careers as art directors. That's a great way to learn how to tell a story visually. In a 30-second spot, that's a very powerful tool to have at your disposal. You've also got to work well with talent and know a lot about every role and every craft going on around you. They're all there to help you get what you're looking for, so you need to know what you want in the frame, and how to get it.

Q: In the commercial world of directing, how much creative freedom do you have beyond an agency creative brief?

A: I'm lucky in that the majority of my work comes from the television side. Traditionally, ad agencies give a director a fully realized set of storyboards and ask you to put your stamp on it. If you're lucky, you can make a great contribution, but many times you're just asked to 'shoot the board'. In the television world, we're brought in at the beginning of a project to help develop ideas for a campaign. Sometimes it's collaboration with the network and other times we're competing with other creative agencies where the best idea wins the job.

Q: How do you typically get hired besides word of mouth and past relationships?

A: Our relationships and word of mouth are really how we *do* get hired. Repeat business is great because it validates your work and shows you've done a good job for your client. Word of mouth is also validating, because it means people are talking about you in a favorable light. Your work is causing buzz.

Q: How are commercial directors compensated?

A: Directors are usually compensated by a day rate based on how many days are spent on set. Sometimes they also share in profit from the cost of production. My day rate can fluctuate wildly based on the project's budget.

Q: What role, if any does technology play in your job today?

A: Technology is hugely important today just as every filmmaker needs to know what the hot new camera will do or what the latest shooting technique is. But this is nothing new… it's always been important. D.W. Griffith, Hitchcock and Kubrick all knew what technology they could use to help them visualize their ideas and move them onto the screen.

Q: Tell me something that most people don't know about Glenn Lazzaro?

A: I'm a closet bluegrass musician. I play flat-pick bluegrass guitar. I have a love-hate relationship with bluegrass music. I hate to listen to it but I love to play it! I've always played music and think it's been a great help in my career, because it's gives me another way to communicate ideas.

Q: Glenn, you were somewhat of a pioneer as an all-in-one editor, heavily involved in the development of MTV. Would you mind talking a little bit about that part of your career?

A: It's important to mention that I have a Bachelor of Science in Psychology and never took art or communications in college. That's helped me throughout my career, because to do great things, an editor or director has to know a little about everything: science, art, architecture, music, literature, pop culture, anthropology, and so on. I was lucky to have an exceptionally well-rounded college experience that provided me those tools.

Also, there was a time when I thought I was going to be a working musician, but it never worked out. However, when I started editing, I realized what an advantage I had over other editors because of my musical training and when cutting music videos I was able to communicate with the musicians. I could speak their language; I could talk about rhythm meaningfully. I had already cut hundreds of music videos by the time MTV found me. They said they had seen my name many, many times on slates and wanted to work with the guy that was cutting all their favorite videos.

At MTV back then, all the producers were frustrated with small budgets that didn't allow them to shoot original promo content so they had to repurpose the same footage over and over. As an editor, I was lucky to be there at that time and work with some of the most talented people in the industry. I'd been doing lots of experimental edit room techniques, and MTV totally jumped on it. We started experimenting with how far we could take existing footage and maintain our own MTV signature.

People laugh when I tell this part of the story, but it's true. The biggest advantage I had with footage manipulation was a class I had in high school called *Creative Arts*. Two or three times a semester, we did something entirely different. The teacher wanted to expose us to everything so that we might find the one thing we loved. Pottery, photography, macramé, 8MM animation, silk-screening, block printing.

We learned animation using a B&W Xerox machine. She showed us Nam June Paik's work with magnets and tvs. We built dioramas and put on puppet shows. Years later, I used all these techniques for MTV promos. My co-workers thought I was a genius but I really need a to give credit, thank you Miss Giardina wherever you are!

Q: What was the best time you've ever had working on a project?

A: I think I would say it was shooting a self-funded documentary in NYC and Nashville on bluegrass music. It was so much fun because I met some of my heroes and I was exposed to so many great people that were excited to be part of the story.

Q: What is the most challenging part of your job?

A: Staying relevant is always a big challenge. You can't rest for a second! There is always someone new coming up who wants your job. But the good news is, commercial direction like some other arts is a place that you can remain productive for a long time. Luckily the industry respects experience, so it's not a big deal every year when my birthday rolls around.

Q: Have you ever had an intern, or mentored someone? What was the experience like?

A: I have mentored a few editors and it's been a great experience. You learn a lot about yourself, your weaknesses as well as your strengths. The process forces you to put into words into what you do naturally without ever thinking about them. Of course, it's a total pleasure when you help someone and they go on to great success.

Q: Glenn, tell me about your career path.

A: I had a long, successful career as an editor, with no intention of becoming a director. When people asked if I wanted to direct, I was very clear. I'd say, "There are plenty of directors out there; some good, some bad. I'm happy being a good editor that's helping directors be better."

At the time, I'd been making short 'resume' reels for my water ski, surfer and snowboard friends. I'd shoot on a 16MM Bolex and record sound on a mini disc. Then I'd score, edit and mix it all in my edit suite. One day a producer friend watched one of these and said, "Glenn you're already directing." She gave me my first official directing job right there on the spot: a series of network IDs for ESPN. In the middle of shooting with a crew of about 35 really talented people, I thought to myself: "I can't go home. I can't go back to my editor's chair. I love this! I need more." A year later I had my own production company.

Q: What's your best advice for someone aspiring to be a Commercial Director?

A: Total commitment, you have to be all in. Go to sleep thinking about filmmaking, dream about filmmaking, and wake up thinking about filmmaking. That's what I did. I couldn't get enough of the industry. When I started out, my average day went something like this; 7AM to 3PM working in the CBS videotape library; 4PM to 7PM working a free internship at CNN in the World Trade Center; 5PM to 10PM editing wedding videos for a company in Staten Island called *Moving Memories*. On Saturdays I would shoot weddings for them and then I'd edit on Sundays. I've never regretted the hard work or those long hours for one moment.

Another amazing person I had the pleasure of speaking with is director Sophie Hyde who makes her home in Australia. Sophie is one of a growing number of successful women directors that is bringing her creative muscle to bear in both film and television. Her success with the film *52 Tuesdays* at Sundance has opened up many doors.

SOPHIE HYDE

Director

IMDB - 52 Tuesdays, Sam Klemke's Time Machine, Animals

Q: Sophie, what drew you to making documentary type films?

A: When I started University, the first presentation I had to give was on documentary film and I was exposed to Michael Apted's *7-Up* series and I and became immediately fascinated by documentary as a form – what it offered and also the problematic nature of it. I've been very lucky to be let into the lives of many different people; the fact that you can sit down with someone for an interview and get into a long conversation about things that would normally be difficult to talk about is a great privilege. It's one the greatest pleasures of my working life.

Q: *52 Tuesdays* was your dramatic feature directorial debut and you won Sundance, an incredible achievement. Would you highlight your path to directing this film? I assume it's not as simple as one day directing a commercial, and the next a feature.

A: No it's not. I've been making films for 15 years and earning my living entirely from it for 10. I started working as a producer's assistant but I felt frustrated at the way films seemed to be made. I didn't enjoy the hierarchical structure, or the seeming lack of creative space. It's an industrial model that works for efficiency but wasn't the way I wanted to work.

For many years I made videos for nightclubs, theatre and dance shows and worked alongside artists from other art forms to make shows with regional kids and things like that. At the same time my partner and I (Bryan Mason who is the cinematographer/editor) started to make documentaries for tv and some short films.

All our films were well-received and won prizes but none of them broke out or went on to one of the top tier festivals. In 2010 we joined forces with documentary filmmaker Matt Bate and Closer Productions in its current form was created. Together we made two feature docs *Life in Movement*, which I co-wrote, co-directed and produced and, *Shut Up Little Man! An Audio Misadventure*, which I produced, then came *52 Tuesdays*.

We are essentially collaborators making stuff together and shift roles on different projects depending on the project need, our wants and what we are good at or can offer to the production.

Q: Do women who wish to become film vs. face any special challenges in the film industry?

A: Yes it's quite clear that they do. We all know the Hollywood stats - only 4 % of films are directed by women and the Cannes Film festival has terrible stats for numbers of female who directed films in competition and the fact that only one woman has ever won the Best Director Oscar.

In Australia only 16% of films are directed by women and of the films released in the cinema in Australia (from around the world) only 12% are directed by women. I see this as a problem.

Women are not an "alternate voice" or minority, we are 50% of the population. I think we need to counter the problem. It's not just about equality in the workforce, but rather that we reflect, challenge and reinforce our worldview through our stories; we have been limiting the perspective of these things.

The reasons for these problems are varied, but I believe that one reason is that women seem more likely to show their reservations in their abilities, to question themselves out-loud and to express their doubts.

As women we are always taught that the answer lies in us, to show our strength and to show that we have no doubts, and that we should lead with absolute certainty – apparently that's how we will get the jobs. For me, this is problematic – I don't necessarily think I would have faith in a job applicant who expressed no doubt about themselves at all – and yet I often feel that is what we are being told as women.

For me, questioning and doubt are a part of what I do and they are tools to be trained and used in my work. Perhaps if we were to start to value a broader range of directing styles and a broader range of stories we might start to see more diversity and a richer scope of stories.

Q: How long did you spend in preproduction prior to shooting the first frame of *52 Tuesdays*?

A: We were developing the film since 2009 while we made our two other feature docs and we started shooting in August 2010. In terms of full time preproduction, we didn't have all that long. Once we started shooting we were constantly in a state of writing, preproduction, production and post.

Q: Has winning at Sundance allowed you to connect at levels that were not accessible to you before? If so, please tell us about it.

A: Yes - more people have seen the film and I've had the opportunity to connect with more filmmakers as well as a larger audience. Attending festivals and doing Q&A's as part of a release are still some of my favorite things to do. Also, there are some people who will have meetings with me who may not have before which is nice, crazy, but nice.

Q: Funding … always hard and many times impossible. How do you fund your films?

A: We are fortunate in Australia to have government support. We rely on a mixture of government funding and sales.

Generally in Australia to access any government investment you have to have a domestic distributor and an international sales agent already attached. For *52* we didn't a distributor or agent so we were funded through very innovative programs from the South Australian Film Corporation (SAFC) and Screen Australia. These programs were equally about taking risks and developing Australian voices, in particular the FILMLAB programs through the

SAFC.

We were also supported in all of our films by the very excellent folks at the Adelaide Film Festival, who have an investment fund for Australian films and have commissioned a range of very interesting work.

I should also note that to survive, our company makes a lot of other screen work as well – corporate films and arts projects and the like.

Q: What was the best time you have ever had working on a film?

A: Making long form is very satisfying. My favorite thing these days is working with the rest of our team to dissect and challenge each other's films in the early stages of writing and again in the edit suite. Working on these ideas in the story room is a lot of fun because early on everything is so filled with potential.

Another area of enjoyment for me personally is working with the cast; on *52* we shared a wild, raw extended time together. I also feel very privileged to interview people and gain insight into their lives when making a documentary. At the end of the day I'm exhausted and don't have a lot of personal time but am grateful because each film teaches me a lot about how I want to work, and how I want to live.

Q: What advice might you like to pass along?

A: Focus on your work, get good at it, and be rigorous about what you think and whether it works for both you and for your audience. Also, be original - find a way of telling a story that is unique to you alone.

Q: Is there any one person in particular that was instrumental in helping your career?

A: Many people but specifically my partner Bryan Mason. Working with Bryan has been a partnership in the truest and most full sense, we always decide things together and work toward them feeling our way, guiding each other, challenging each other and taking on the weight when the other can't. We have very different skills and we don't always agree but without Bryan I'm sure I would have taken a different path and I'm not sure I would had ever had the courage to pursue directing.

Q: Have you ever had an intern, or mentored someone? What was the experience like?

A: In many ways I have informally mentored people and been mentored myself. Currently I work closely with a writer/producer/director Matthew Vesely. He has worked with us in the story room and as a development assistant and he has a wonderful brain for story and so the mentorship is not one sided. I am now producing his short film!

Q: What's your take on the future of filmmaking and its integration in the digital world i.e.: YouTube, Streaming, Interactive TV, that type of thing?

A: The great thing is the opportunity for filmmakers to be directly connected to their audience and provide relatively niche work to interested people anywhere.
At the moment it's still hard to walk the line between more traditional modes of distribution, where there are experts getting your films out to audiences in each territory. You can feel quite removed from the process and this broader (but smaller in each place) release where you engage directly.

For me, the attraction of being connected to the audience is that I love to talk about the ideas during the development and again when they are released. For *52 Tuesdays* we had this film that could play in cinemas and on small screens but we also created a participatory project called *My 52 Tuesdays*, which was available for free as a smartphone app. People had an opportunity to answer a question from us each week and in doing so create their own portrait of their year (or their own *52 Tuesdays*). This enabled us to take the themes we were exploring and give new life and an experiential component to our filmmaking. I don't know what this means financially but as a maker it's an incredibly satisfying and creates ongoing dialogue.

FIRST ASSISTANT DIRECTOR

Who is the person the director counts on most to make sure the working environment for the crew is awesome and the film's entire production is completed on schedule and on budget? It's obvious given the heading for this section and *yes* it's the First Assistant Director!

I may have oversimplified the responsibilities a bit but the first assistant director is the Go To person for just about everything during production including directing scenes when the film's director deems necessary.

I had the great pleasure of speaking to the mighty Bruce Moriarty, one of the most sought after first assistant directors in the entire film industry. He was certainly a hard fellow to pin down as he schedules back-to-back productions years in advance. I was lucky enough to catch him between blockbusters!

BRUCE MORIARTY

First Assistant Director

IMDB - Forest Gump, The Amazing Spiderman, Transformers, Man of Steel, Batman vs. Superman, Bolden!

Q: Bruce, Would you tell me exactly what you do as the 1st Assistant Director?

A: The job of 1st assistant director entails the initial organization of the film with regard to scheduling the scenes that make up the film in a day-to-day format that best allows for both the creative process and financial considerations of the project. I am also responsible for bringing together all the elements that support the requirements of the story including the actors, stunts, extras, and the many different departments that contribute on a daily basis.

Another important role I take on is making sure that we work in a safe manner and in a safe environment. This means that we rehearse difficult stunts and check all special effects ahead of time to ensure that; number one they work, and two that they work safely. An example would be the many car stunts that were performed in the *Spider-Man 2* film with no injuries. The only victims were the large number of vehicles we destroyed to achieve a very exciting chase sequence.

Q: You have a long track record of successful films, what personal traits do you credit for your longevity in what is an extremely competitive business?

A: I believe that first and foremost it's because I always treat the cast and crew with respect and never allow myself to become a screaming tyrant on the set. In addition my main role on any given film is to assist the director in achieving his vision and committing it to film. I have dedicated myself to this endeavor. For the most part, my relationships with the different directors has allowed me to collaborate creatively, which for me has been a big plus in my outlook on the job.

Q: Working at the highest level in our industry, might you recall a few stepping stones that brought you to where you are today?

A: Happenstance! I started out as a horse trainer/wrangler/stuntman on such films as the *Black Stallion*. A friend of mine was looking for a 2nd assistant director on a project and offered me the job. I wasn't working at the time so I said, "Yes!" and continued to move up the ladder to where I am today while still training horses and doing stunt work along the way.

Q: Is there any specific reason you never pursued being a 'Director'?

A: That's a tough question but I suppose the short answer would be

'Opportunity'. There are horses for courses and I'm still training mine!

Q: Bruce, what's the most unpleasant part of your job?

A: That's an easy one. Being on the road and away from home for long periods of time can take its toll on other parts of your life. Another thing would be standing out on a set in the cold and the rain, or even worse, working in the cold and rain at night!

Q: How does a 1st Assistant Director like yourself get paid, and are there residuals, etc.?

A: I am a member of the 'Directors Guild of America' and the 'Directors Guild of Canada' so I get paid per the negotiated contract and yes we do receive residuals.

Q: Tell me something that most people don't know about being a 1st Assistant Director?

A: How much work the 1st assistant director actually does in the planning of a film prior to shooting. Properly prepping a film is key and you can put in some very long hours, sometimes up to 16 hours a day and 6 days a week.

Q: What was the best time you've ever had working on a film and why?

A: There have been so many good times. *Forrest Gump* was a standout because as we were making the film everyone on the cast and crew knew we were making something very special that would be enjoyed by many and stand the test of time. It is a real classic.

Man of Steel was also a great project to be involved with it because it was another chance to reboot a franchise. Working with Zack Snyder was amazing as his sense of knowing what he wanted to achieve was refreshing. He even draws his own storyboards! What's written on the pages comes alive through his drawings and is always better, a real step above.

Casino Royale was another film that I very much enjoyed working and collaborating with director Martin Campbell. Rebooting the James Bond franchise with Daniel Craig while achieving an 'on schedule' film that shot in five countries.

Q: Is it possible to live outside of California and still be a successful player in the film industry?

A: I would say yes. I have managed to have a fairly productive career in the industry even though my wife, Jill and I live full time on our ranch in Banner, Wyoming.

Q: Is there any one person that was instrumental in helping your career?

A: I'd have to thank a few people including 2nd Unit Director/Stunt Coordinator, Glen Randall. Glen hired me to do the *Black Stallion* film and many others as a horse trainer/wrangler/stunt man and assistant director. There was also director, John Irvin who gave me first job as 1st AD on a film called *Next Of Kin*. Also, director, Martin Campbell has hired me on some great films, one being *Casino Royale*.

Q: Have you ever had an intern, or mentored someone?

A: It seems on every project I manage to take someone under my wing and help them move forward in our industry. It's always rewarding to see that they are doing well and using what they learned to further their careers.

Q: Bruce, is there anything you've not accomplished that's still on your personal list?

A: I would like to make a film in New Zealand. I have many friends in the industry there and really they enjoy the country. I almost made a film that was to shoot in New Zealand and in China but it didn't happen.

Q: What's your take on the future of film making and it's integration in the digital world i.e. YouTube, Streaming, Interactive TV, that type of thing?

A: I think that with all the different venues that exist today there are opportunities for anyone who wants to work in industry provided they are willing to put body and soul into whatever path they choose to take.

Q: Is there anything else you would like us to know about the 1st Assistant Directors job?

A: The job is as rewarding as you make it … to know that you've contributed to something that millions of people will see and hopefully enjoy is something very special.

PRODUCTION DESIGNER

With the script developed (or in development) let's turn our focus to the visual components of a film. What will our film look like and how will it feel aesthetically to the viewer? The production designer will work very closely with the film's director, producer and director of photography to create the overall feel of the visual environment of the film.

The production designer typically guides a large creative team in the art department that includes the Art Director, Costume Designer, Special Effects, Makeup, Construction and so forth.

Marc Fisichella is one of Hollywood's top Production designers and has worked on some of the industry's most successful theatrical releases. I had a chance to catch him not long after he wrapped *The Maze Runner.*

MARC FISICHELLA

Production Designer

IMDB - The Maze Runner, The Last Days of Summer, X-Men, Deep Water Horizon

Q: Marc, you recently completed work on the film "Maze Runner" and the world you created is quite unique. How much of this comes from the director's vision and how much is created in your own mind?

A: After reading the script and any other source material, in this case, James Dashner's novel, I came up with visuals and references and create sketches to present to the director. Using that as a starting point we begin to sculpt the look of the movie. Ideally, our visions will complement and inspire each other. Sometimes you discover that a director's vision is far in another direction or perhaps he or she has trouble communicating or expressing a vision in which case my job as a designer becomes much tougher.

In the case of *The Maze Runner*, the director Wes Ball and I were relatively in the same galaxy. My intent was to not over design this film. With material such as *The Maze Runner*, you are essentially starting from scratch and could easily overindulge in design and eclipse the story. But by keeping everything in a realm that we can visually understand and relate to, the unbelievable, becomes believable.

Q: At what point in Preproduction are you typically brought in, and what might you be doing?

A: Usually I am brought onto a project once a project is 'green-lit' or approved by the studio. Depending of the size of the project, my allotted time to design the film is anywhere from 10 to 20 weeks prior to the start of principle photography and I would continue my work through the completion of photography which can be another 10-12 weeks.

Sometimes, though, as in the case with films like *The Maze Runner,* I begin working with the director early on to conceptualize the film in broad strokes to determine what kind of budget would be needed to make the film and make decisions on where the film should be shot. It is also during that time we determine if its even possible to make the movie for the budget the studio wants to spend.

Q: How much does someone in your position need to know about the latest and greatest technology when you are designing a production?

A: I started my career hand drawing with a pencil. You really had to be a fine artist to produce drawings that would sell your ideas and concepts. We would have an ammonia based blueprint machine in the office to make our blue prints. The smell was strong and the fumes would burn your eyes but nothing looked as official as an actual blueprint of your drawings. However, most people, including directors and producers couldn't always interpret blueprints visually.

Today, with programs like *Sketchup* and *Modo* we can render our ideas and designs quickly and easily in 3D and actually move through the digital models. And now with large format color printers being commonplace in the art department, we can render our drawings in full size and full color which is ideal for presentations.

Though I love working with these tools, I still begin with a very crude foam model of the set that I would likely build my self. I will build it manipulate it, rip it apart, add on to it until I can start to see my vision materialize in the scale and proportion that I want. This physical model, though crude, becomes my guide for creating the 3D computer renderings that will then eventually become working drawings for the construction department.

Q: What special skill set is required to be successful as a Production Designer, beyond having a good eye and attention to detail?

A: As a production designer, it is important to have the ability to sketch. Many production designers who have come up through a computer design path may have a good eye but lack the basic skill of pencil drawing. There is no easier way for people to understand what you visualize in your head than to quickly sketch it on paper to have everyone to see it as you do. It's amazing to me that we have all this visual technology but some of my greatest design moments were created on a napkin while eating lunch during a location scout with the director.

Q: Do you work as a sub-contractor, or as an employee for a production company?

A: Once I am hired onto a project, I become an employee of the company. It's a company that will only exist during the making of the film. Once the project is completed most everyone on the film join the ranks of the unemployed. But by then, a break is always welcome.

Q: Marc, would you talk about how Production Designers are compensated?

A: I used to joke with this producer who couldn't help but hover over the set designers in the art department watching them draw. He would ask them questions about what sets cost and say, "Does it have to be that big?" I pulled him aside and said, "All you need to know is this. If you here the sound of an electric pencil sharpener then its going to cost you money. If you hear the sounds of the electric erasers then you are saving money." We don't get paid by the drawing or by the set or even by the hour.

Production designers and art directors get paid a flat fee by the week. Very long weeks that sometimes run 60 to 80 hours. We get paid the same every week no matter how much we work. And we almost always take our work home with us at the end of the day and on weekends. There never seems to be enough time to do what you need to do.

Q: You've worked as an Art Director, Set Designer and now Production Designer. What is the difference between the positions and who reports to whom?

A: The head of the art department is the production designer. He or she conceives the visual style of the film. The production designer has one or multiple art directors to oversee the construction of the sets and manage the set designers who physically draw the working plans of the sets under the guidance of the production designer. These drawings or plans are what the construction department uses to construct the sets. Art directors also track the spending of each set to keep construction on budget.

Q: Tell me something that most people don't know about you, Marc?

A: Most people don't know how to spell my name! But really, I have this secret aspiration to open a restaurant. Not that I want to run a restaurant but I really want to design a restaurant that is more of a visual and sensory experience than anything else. I could care less about the food.

Q: Could you give us a brief summary of your path to Production Designer?

A: I attended film school on the east coast with the aspirations of becoming a director and after graduation I landed a job at a commercial production house in Boston working on commercials. I did pretty much what ever was needed from making coffee to loading film magazines.

Everything we shot was against the ugly the brick walls and corners of our studio. No thought was put into the sets for these spots. I started designing and sketching ideas for sets for commercials we were bidding on. I included a rough budget and submitted them to the producers. It was my way of standing out from the other entry level employees with vague job descriptions.

I suddenly found myself the 'In House' production designer and even got a small raise. Very small! After a couple of years I headed to Los Angeles to break into feature films where I started as a set dresser and always carried my drawings and sketches with me. I would show them to production designers on the projects I worked on. One day I got a break and was asked to art direct a tv movie called *Prime Target*. From that point the projects got bigger and I built a resume, got an agent and took a lot of meetings because I had a lot of free time. The hard part of this business is getting your first job. The only thing harder is getting your second job.

Q: Do you travel the globe as a Production Designer?

A: I travel a great deal. When I started in the film business I lived in Los Angeles because that's where you have to be to get established. In the past most movies were filmed in Los Angeles and quite a few went on location to other states or countries usually depending on what the local of the script called for.
Today most films shoot in states other than California as a result of rebates and tax incentives offered by competing states. These incentives take precedent over shooting in a place that offers the best look for a film and that makes the job of the production designer much more challenging.

Q: Would you share one of the *'good times'* you've had on a film?

A: I did a film called *The Man Without A Face* directed by Mel Gibson. We shot the film in Rockport, Maine. It was beautiful location with a great script and excellent producers who knew how to make a film the right way. Nothing seemed to go wrong throughout the production. That almost never happens in our business.

Q: There are challenges associated with every type of job, tell me about yours.

A: As production designers, we create or sometimes recreate these massive settings on limited budgets with tight schedules. Sets have to be cinematically appealing, historically accurate and shootable. In other words, can a film crew of about a hundred people work within the boundaries of the sets you have created and achieve what they need to do in terms of lighting, shooting and blocking.

Anna and the King is a great example of trying to create an environment true to the history and the story. The movie's Grand Royal Palace and grounds were created from the ground up. We cleared land near Ipoh, Malaysia to build the massive 'practical' set, meaning we built it full scale and the only visual FX we used were to add in the spectacular roof on the Great Hall for extreme wide shots.

At the time, the studio was under a lot of pressure to start shooting by a certain date. We had very little time to plan and construct the 30-acre set and the amount of detail to recreate The Grand Palace was overwhelming. We had thousands of people working around the clock constructing, sculpting painting and landscaping while dealing with severe weather, flooding and deadly pythons that lived amongst the vegetation all around us. We were actually still constructing the set as the shooting crew began filming the palace.

Q: Do you use PA's or interns?

A: Art department PAs are the entry-level position. We generally don't use interns but I always make sure I give an opportunity for our PAs to step up and contribute creatively and its great to work with fresh and enthusiastic talent.

Q: Advice for an aspiring Production Designer?

A: Get into the camera department, it's much cleaner and there is a lot more respect. Seriously though, work your way up. Don't skip a step. Be a set dresser, set designer, work as an asst. Art director and observe everything along the way. You are part of a film crew making a movie and not just an interior designer.

What you do affects just about everything else in the movie including how a DP lights the scene, how a director blocks the actors, the colors a costume designer will use, and most importantly, your sets will tell the back story of the characters. Be observant, detail oriented and most importantly learn how to collaborate.

Q: Marc, is there anything else you would like us to know about you or the job of a Production Designer?

A: The politics, the compromise; you have to be prepared for compromise. We think of ourselves as artists but making movies is a business and decisions are made based on the bottom line. Your job as a production designer is not only to create a world and a look for a movie, but you also have to create environments that function in a way that a director, a director of photography, the shooting crew and actors can navigate in ways that enhance their contribution to the creative process.

I spend a lot of my time working with the first assistant director on creating a workable shooting schedule because we may have to deliver sets that work for an actor's schedule. As problems arise during shooting, the production designer is often called upon to help solve them.

Dan Leigh is another prominent Production Designer who started as a theater designer before moving to a very successful career in feature films.

DAN LEIGH
Production Designer

IMDB - Warrior, Person of Interest, John Wick, The Outskirts, Eternal Sunshine of the Spotless Mind, Gypsy

Q: Dan, you worked on *John Wick*, a film I liked very much. Would you explain the relationship between yourself, the director and other department heads? I understand it can be quite complicated.

A: *JOHN WICK* is more a fable than grounded in reality. Dark, yes, but timeless in it's place in the world; it's imagining *"what if..."* The canvas is a combination of classic New York environments fused with contemporary elements, and trendy New York spiced with old-school criminal elements.

This film had two opposing directors, which meant two opinions for everything. filmmaking needs firm decisions to move forward so preproduction was frustrating for everyone. Collaboration was nearly impossible - if I brought an idea to the table, only one director would respond. There was simply no collaboration with both directors at the same time over the same idea.

If good movies are about good storytelling, the production period had most of us concerned. The cinematographer brought a music video sensibility and the gifted editor, Elisabet Ronaldsdóttir, managed to glue it all together.

Q: You seem to be very comfortable jumping back and forth between feature film and television production. Tell me about the differences.

A: Feature film is a director's medium. Episodic tv is a creator/writer/producer medium.

Feature film design entails in-depth discussions with the director, period. Research is compiled and examined by the two of us with very little input from anyone else.

Design for episodic television happens between the designer and an ever-expanding number of executive producers, network/cable executives, show creators, show runners, and lastly, a director or two. TV design requires significant presentations of design concepts and materials that are discussed at length by scores of people on two coasts.

There are also significant differences between feature film production and tv production regarding time. Even with today's reduced preproduction periods and budgets, feature production is slower, more methodical and more planned out than episodic tv production.

During the first season of *Person of Interest* I often said that episodic tv is *Iron Chef* for Designers. While one episode is filming, the next episode is in preproduction. The camera rolls everyday and sets have to be ready at break-neck speed to make an hour of television every eight days.

Q: What does a Production Designer do and what exactly are your responsibilities?

A: Imagine a film or television still frame, frozen in front of you. In your mind, remove the actors from the frame. Now look at what remains – everything else that you see falls to the production designer; i.e. a train station, the train, the luggage, the steam, the taxis, the trash, the signs, the posters, the tickets, the cigarette butts, a leaky pipe, a few pigeons; in other words, everything that's not the actor. The production designer's task is so large and all-encompassing that it's almost incomprehensible to the audience.

And, of course, there's a heavy responsibility to stay within a budget. As materials become more expensive and labor rates climb, budgets have not really increased to reflect higher costs. It is increasingly more difficult to deliver a director's vision within the current budget restrictions.

Q: What are the traits of a skilled Production Designer?

A: A production designer has to be a good boss. There are scores of people working under the production designer - every one has a skill set and specific task that is essential for the look of the film to succeed. I have the utmost respect for my staff and crew and it is my responsibility to keep morale high and energy up and in the current climate of diminishing budgets, a happy energized crew carries me a long way.

Q: Dan, you went from Rock and Roll to Feature Films - tell us how you got here!

A: I arrived in New York, intending a career as a stage designer. There were designs for Regional Theatre, off-Broadway, and The Kennedy Center and a brief Rock-n-Roll period for MEATLOAF, SCORPIONS, and a KISS tour to Australia.

It was my friend and mentor, Stuart Wurtzel, who brought me into the film world. I worked with him for several years as an assistant and un-credited Art director on projects including *The Purple Rose of Cairo* and *Hannah and Her Sisters* for Woody Allen so in a way, I did have art direction experience before my first Production Design project.

Q: What has been one of your greatest experiences so far?

A: The best time for me was *A Walk on the Moon* shot north of Montreal. We were filming over a summer in a beautiful area in the mountains. This was Tony Goldwyn's first film as director, and both Liev Schreiber and Viggo Mortensen were relatively unknown. We were far away from the NY or LA pressure cooker and the work was easily collaborative. It was a wonderful way to work and the results are captured on screen.

Q: Do you find yourself getting involved with a project on an emotional level like a director might?

A: One of the best and most interesting aspects of production design is being allowed into places that most people can't access. I've had the unique privilege to see private homes and apartments of every income level; high-powered businesses and crumbling ruins, and it's a kind of Social Anthropology that comes with the job. The most challenging projects have to do with the emotional impact that some locations have on me personally. It is important for me to connect with the screenplay in a meaningful way *emotionally* – very similar to an actor's process. It's my job to create a world that honestly conveys tone, character, and emotion in concert with the cast.

It was difficult to stand at the fence where Mathew Shepard was beaten and left to die, but *The Laramie Project* required my full attention. It was difficult to spend an afternoon walking through the US Military Mortuary at Dover Air Force Base, but *Taking Chance* required the research trip to recreate the facility. Very challenging, indeed, but these moments will change you. *The Laramie Project* changed some minds and *Taking Chance* changed US Military policy regarding the remains of those fallen in service to our country. The personal challenges fall away when the project takes on a greater meaning.

Q: Would you mind passing on your best advice to the next generation of production designers?

A: Listen. Train yourself to listen. To truly collaborate, you must listen to writers, directors, producers, cinematographers, production managers, visual fx supervisors, stunt coordinators, etc. If you listen to them, they will usually listen to you, and that's true collaboration. Part of production design is solving the problems of other departments and you have to know what those problems are.

Q: Any closing remarks, Dan?

A: Feature films and tv productions aren't designed in studios or offices at desks or drafting tables; *they're designed in vans*. Yes, vans - scouting vans. The scouting van is where the designer forges relationships with the director, the cinematographer, the producer and the location manager.

The scouting van is the petri dish where wants and ideas are discussed as locations are accepted or rejected. What happens in the scouting van shapes a production more than any meeting at an office or studio. Often even casting happens in that van. Production designers spend a tremendous amount of time riding in scouting vans. So, in that van you should listen very carefully.

TALENT AGENT

When I was in the planning stage of writing this book I explored various ways of connecting with influential people whom I thought might be willing to share their personal views, real world experience, and deliver some actionable value. While this may not seem all that hard, it proved to be a tough assignment as I hit numerous roadblocks along the way that delayed my progress and goal of publishing in a timely manner.

Although I can't share my secret for locating and connecting with the top crew members in the film industry I can tell you that most of these people have managers and talent agents. They are the gatekeepers that find opportunities for their clients as well as filter inquires (such as mine) so their clients don't get caught up in the business side, and are allowed to focus on the creative endeavors for which they are hired.

ROCCO HINDMAN

President and CEO

Sandra *Marsh & Associates*

Q: Rocco, as a talent agent for Line Producers, Production Designers, Costume Designers, DPs, and Editors what might you be doing on a typical day?

A: My day involves countless conversations with producers, studio production executives, line producers, production managers, and directors to discuss their upcoming productions and to convince them to take meetings with - and ultimately hire - my clients.

I also advise my clients with regard to prospective employment opportunities and strategize with them about their careers in general. When a client is offered a job I would also negotiate the terms of employment and mediate any issues or conflicts that arise during the engagement.

Q: Is representing film crews different than if I were an agent for actors and actresses?

A: I think the fundamental job of an agent is fairly consistent across all specialties, whether representing actors, cinematographers, writers, or directors. The agent is expected to help procure employment opportunities and to negotiate the terms of the engagement. As for any peculiarities of representing below-the-line talent, I am sure there are several; due to the unique roles my clients perform in the overall production process as compared to other talent.

For example, we tend to deal with projects that have already been 'green-lit' or are close to being green-lit (i.e., approved by the financier to proceed into preproduction and production).

My clients do not typically have to wait through the lengthy development process, nor are they expected to commit to a project long before it is a "go" so we spend less time waiting for projects to come to fruition than an actor, writer, or director might be required to.

Furthermore, because the work of my various clients spans all phases of preproduction, production, and postproduction, it is important that I'm familiar with the relevant people and processes associated therewith. A below-the-line agent has to be knowledgeable about the technical areas that relate to his particular clients.

Q: Would you briefly tell us about your career path?

A: My path into agency life started from a fascination with filmmaking in general. I attended film school for both undergraduate and graduate studies, culminating in a Master of Fine Arts degree in Cinema & Television Production.

As an undergraduate, I also pursued a minor study in Business Administration, including Entertainment Law classes, because the business side of the film industry interested me almost as much as the creative elements at that time. Like many of my peers, immediately after college, while continuing to produce and direct short films for little or no money, I took a variety of entry-level freelance jobs on television and film productions.

In 1998, while I was working in the art department of the feature film, *The Green Mile*, the production designer, Terence Marsh, introduced me to his wife (and agent), Sandra, who was looking for an agent trainee for her agency. After meeting, she offered me the position, and for the next two years I worked closely with her and the other agents until I was promoted to agent. I have been with the same company for more than 16 years.

Q: I'm sure you spend a lot of time on the phone, is it cold calling, or are you typically contacted for the talent you represent?

A: The conversations that I have are the result of both "cold" calls that I place and inquiries I receive from producers and directors. While it is quite common to receive inquiries about specific clients or general requests for crew suggestions for an upcoming production, many of the projects that I follow come about through direct inquiries that I initiate.

I hesitate to use the phrase "cold calling" often, because I usually have an established rapport with many of the individuals I speak to about projects. In that respect, the information comes about through ongoing conversations that are anything but cold. That said, there are always inquiries that must be made of people that I have rarely, if ever, spoken to before, so I do still conduct a considerable amount of new inquiries in search of leads. Our agency also has a designated person whose primary responsibility is to contact producers and production companies to ascertain information about projects in development and preproduction.

Q: How are agents compensated?

A: Talent agencies receive a fixed percentage of their clients' gross salaries as compensation for services rendered. The industry standard for below-the-line talent in the

US is ten percent (10%), which is paid to the agency by the client, and the agency compensates the individual agent from that sum.

Compensation of agents varies from agency to agency. Some agents receive a base salary as a draw against a percentage of the commissions collected from their clients while others receive a fixed salary plus periodic discretionary bonuses. Some agencies reward their agents with signing bonuses for bringing a new client into the agency or a share of the commissions earned by a specific client brought to the agency. There are no hard and fast rules.

Q: Do you travel as part of your job?

A: Yes, my work requires networking and face time with clients, prospective clients, and their potential employers. As such, it is quite common to travel to the major film festivals to see new films before they have a theatrical release and to scope out the work of the key crew on those films. Set visits, both locally and afar, are an important part of building and maintaining a network and provide the agent an opportunity to observe a client's work firsthand. Other common activities include business lunches and attendance at premieres and film screenings. We also frequently attend awards presentations sponsored by the various unions and guilds that represent our clients.

Q: Tell me something that most people don't know about you?

A: Often when I am reading an exceptional screenplay, I will intentionally not read the last 30 pages, in order to preserve something for the movie-going experience.

Q: What is the best part of being a Talent Agent?

A: The moments that I enjoy the most are those times when my client and I, after much effort, succeed in securing a break-through opportunity. An example could be a first major feature film or simply a project that takes the client's career in a new and exciting direction. In those moments, it is nearly impossible not to share a client's enthusiasm for what has been accomplished and what lies ahead.

Q: Have you ever had the chance to mentor someone?

A: Despite my busy schedule, I try to stay involved with students and recent graduates of my undergraduate school, Ohio University, in particular. Through this connection, I have assisted a small number of aspiring filmmakers and young professionals to transition into the entertainment industry after college, across a wide range of interests.

Some have gone on to pursue careers in editing or cinematography, others now work at major production companies, and one of them even works here at the agency with me, where he tracks upcoming projects for us on a daily basis.

I find that the experience of mentoring relies on the drive of the person seeking to be mentored. The most productive and enjoyable experiences I have had in this regard have always been with young people who had a clear idea of what they would like to achieve, were realistic in their expectations, and took the initiative to maintain the relationship.

Q: What is the profile of a successful Talent Agent?

A: Above all a successful agent must have good people skills. Agents must interact with an array of challenging personalities every day, including the mighty and the meek. Agents are negotiators, counselors, mediators, advocates, life coaches, and problem-solvers all in one.

To be truly effective, an agent must sincerely believe in the client and feel that the client stands out in some way. A knack for being persistent but not clumsy or pushy is a great asset, in my opinion as well as the ability to find creative solutions to conventional problems.

Q: On a personal level Rocco, what's the toughest part of your job?

A: One of the most challenging parts of the job is the amount of time it requires. With a roster of international clients and a slate of films shooting all around the world, the work of an agent knows no set schedule. Outside of regular business hours, there are screenplays to read, films and tv productions to watch, e-mails and phone calls to return, and deals to make. Rarely is there a vacation or long holiday weekend that doesn't still require work to be done. This can take a toll on one's personal life and relationships, if an effort isn't made to preserve some sense of personal time when possible.

Q: The million-dollar question … for someone starting out in the film industry that aspires to be talent agent, how might they get their foot in the door?

A: I would recommend that they seek introductions to a few agents working the area(s) of most interest and ask for a brief informational interview. If you have difficulty getting access to an agent for this purpose, try connecting with a junior agent or even an agent trainee at an agency that interests you.

Think carefully about your interest in this line of work and be honest with yourself about your reasons for pursuing a career as an agent. It takes a significant amount of time and effort to establish key relationships and build your reputation as an agent, regardless of how well respected the agency that employs you may be.

If you still decide to pursue such a career, be open-minded about your possibilities and apply for an entry-level position at an agency where you can begin to learn the trade. Expect to start at the bottom and to put your time in before other opportunities may be presented. Many people drop out of the agency scene after just a few months or even a year. Endurance is essential to progress.

ART DIRECTOR

The largest department on most feature films is the art department, which is headed by the production designer. The person that works directly with and for the production designer is the art director, who is tasked with the project management of set construction and responsible for delivering on the vision of the production designer as well as managing the budget.

Many departments and film crews work with and under the direction of the art director, including the storyboard artists, draughtsman, construction, set decorators, special efx, and many others. An art director in the film industry needs to have a diverse set of skills and they must be able to conceptualize ideas, understand basic construction, communicate well with other departments, and have a well-rounded knowledge of architecture, and interior design.

One of the busiest Art directors in Hollywood is Mark Scruton. Originally from the UK, Mark has vision, dedication, and talent… lots of talent!

MARK SCRUTON

Senior Art Director

IMDB - Gravity, Fury, Jupiter Ascending, Pan, Jason Bourne, Ready Player One

Q: Mark; let's talk about what an Art Director does in the film world?

A: The job of an art director can vary widely from project to project. Primarily our job is to realize the visual environment of a film as envisioned by the production designer. This means we have to be part architect, part interior designer, part historian and part project manager whilst having a good understanding of the filmmaking process and narrative structure. As a senior or supervising art director this also includes managing budgets, schedules & the art department crew.

For instance, on the film *Fury* my job was to design and oversee the construction of a complete German town, which we built on an abandoned airfield near Watford, England. The town would form the middle act of the film and represent a significant financial commitment on the part of the production company. Because of this, and its overall scale it needed it's own dedicated team. On other productions such as *Jupiter Ascending* I may be required to look after several different sets such as spaceship interiors and futuristic refineries.

Q: With whom do you work most closely?

A: Being an art director is very much a collaborative role and you work closely with many different groups all requiring a different approach. First and most importantly is the designer. It's their visions you are implementing and it's important that you understand what they are trying to achieve. The designer will be responding (directly) to the director's wishes so you may also have a direct dialogue with the director as well.

You then have your own art department team. This will consist of assistant art directors, draughts people and other assistants. This team is very dependent on you to keep them fed with work tasks and to ensure there is continuity to the project, and that all models and drawings are correct and appropriate.

Then you have your construction team, which usually consists of carpenters, plasterers and painters all under the control of a construction manager. It is the responsibility of an art director to oversee and guide these trade's people to achieve the desired finishes and to ensure the sets are serviced throughout the filming process.

On some projects you will also need to liaise with sculptors, model makers, metal workers and many other trades all needing guidance and supervision. Good project management skills are a must!

Q: You've worked on so many high profile projects; do you have a personal process for managing all the different aspects of a film?

A: Read the script *twice*. Break the script down, which entails itemizing all the sets that are needed, what happens in them and what they might require.

Sit with the designer and discuss what they envision along with which sets might be locations and which might be builds.

From this information it is then possible to produce a first draft of a budget.

Depending on the schedule you would normally start interviewing and hiring crew at this point. The film could require anywhere from 4 to 40 people, many of whom might require specific skill sets. It's important to put the correct team together as you are dependent on them.

With my team in place I start to develop design ideas using models and illustrations. The designer, director and sometimes the director of Photography will regularly review these.

As this process progresses (and it can go on for a very long time), the budget is refined with the help of the construction manager. Discussions will be held with the producer to understand where the production wants to spend its money and they have final approval over our proposed spend.

The design process is usually dictated by the shooting schedule, which may not be in story order. This means the last set of the film might need to be designed and under construction months before filming even starts.

As the various set designs are approved you begin a program of draughting, whereby the models and illustrations are turned into full sets of architectural drawings. These are then turned over to construction to begin building.

At the same time the set-decorating department will begin to look at how the sets and locations will be dressed with furnishings & props.

Finally, as the sets and locations become ready for filming you would "see in" the shooting crew, ensuring everyone is happy and then oversee any major revamps or story changes as the shooting progresses.

Q: What is the difference between the role of the Senior Art Director and the Supervising Art Director?

A: They can mean different things on different projects. Usually a supervising art director is responsible for budgets, schedules and overseeing the other art directors & crew. On really big films you may also have a senior art director to back up the supervisor and to bring a level of expertise to a project, especially if the film is spread across multiple countries. On smaller films you might have one or the other depending on what level of involvement the designer has, for instance, if they prefer to manage the budget & schedule themselves.

Q: Do you also work closely with the director, cinematographer and producer?

A: As far as the director goes it really depends on them. Some will get involved and spend a lot of time in the art department working with the team, while others will only communicate with the designer. Both approaches have their benefits and pitfalls. It is vital that the supervising art director has a good line of dialogue with the director of photography & the producer. Both need to understand the art department's ideas for a film and both will have their own set of requirements that need to be accommodated.

Q: What are the most important skills an aspiring Art director needs?

A: The two key elements that seem to be very important to being a good art director are flexibility and attention to detail. You never know what the next job will be and what will be required of you as it progresses, so rolling with a situation and being able to adapt at a moment's notice is very important. In the same breath understanding every element of your project, and constantly working to make it as visually interesting as you can, within the constraints you've been given, is crucial.

Q: How do you get hired for a job? Agent, referral, etc.?

A: I have a booking agent and she has introduced me to a lot of people over the years but most of my work these days is acquired through word of mouth.

Q: How are Art directors compensated?
A: We are paid a weekly salary.

Q: What role does technology play in your job?

A: Once upon a time, not that long ago, you would turn up for work with your pencils and set square and be ready to go. However, today, technology is very much at the center of what we do. Things have moved on enormously, predominantly driven by a greater emphasis on presentation and explanation of design proposals and the huge advances in visual effects.

Now, when you arrive for a job you are expected to bring your computer (the more powerful the better,) scanner, graphics tablet, digital camera, laser measure and have software including Autocad, Photoshop, Illustrator, Rhino, Sketchup, Office and even Maya, Zbrush and other more powerful 3D software. Although hand drawings can be beautiful and expressive when well executed, the advancement in design software have benefited the art department as it means we can communicate with vfx, pre-visualization and all other departments, much more effectively.

I've always been interested in vfx and aware of its increasingly important role in film production. However, the real wake up call for me was supervising the movie *Gravity*. This was a film where every shot was an effects shot and everything was to be designed virtually. This was a groundbreaking project and nothing like it had ever been attempted before. Much of the technology involved hadn't even been invented when we started. It gave me a very privileged position of being able to understand and grow as the film developed.

Now, on the other side, it is almost impossible to think of designing without the use of 3D design and draughting technology. Especially now with the introduction of such things as 3D printing it is crucial to keep up with new developments. This can often be a lot harder than it seems though, as the freelance nature of the industry means there is no organized program of training to keep skills up to date, so it is very much on the individual's

76

shoulders.

Q: On the job training?

A: Nearly all the skills I rely on today have been learned on the job. I studied Art Direction at film school and whilst it taught me a lot about how movies are made I soon realized upon leaving, that it had taught me very few of the skills I needed to actually get a job and do the work. I had to do a lot of self-teaching to get the skills I've needed to progress.

Q: Memorable films?

A: I'm lucky to have had some very rewarding experiences on some amazing projects but the best time I ever had was as a concept model maker on *Star Wars: The Phantom Menace* I was still relatively junior at the time and had six amazing (stress free) months making models of all manner of space ships and environments. A situation I had dreamed of since I was five!

I also had an amazing time in India working on the musical *Bride & Prejudice*; it was an extraordinary country and an amazing adventure. Standing in a town square that you've had built with 500 extras and two elephants all performing a choreographed dance routine in the mid day Indian sun, it's hard not to think you've got a pretty cool job!

Q: What is the most challenging part of your job?

A: Trying to pre-empt problems before they happen. Because of the fluidity of movie making and the increasingly rapid turnaround, goalposts often can and do get moved; trying to guess in what direction can drive you to the point of madness. It's very often when you all think you've nailed a set, it's bang on brief and you're all very pleased; then a director comes in and tells you that everything is wrong and not what he wanted at all! At times like that you have to adopt your best poker face, try to ascertain exactly what the problem is, and very quickly come up with a solution. If you're good you'll have several lined up ready to go!

Q: What's your take on the future for Art directors?

A: Art directors will have to be very proactive in the years ahead to keep the role relevant and important. The prevalence of VFX in movies has led to a culture where producers increasingly think that much of what we do can be handled by the vfx department. This couldn't be further from the truth. The role of an art department has always been greater than the sum of its parts. By that I mean that beyond the drawing and model making, art directors and their teams provide a vital role in bringing together all the strands of a production process to ensure that a film has a clear consistent look and that it is produced in an organized and cost effective manner.

Another Art Director working on projects for the big screen as well as television is Lori Agostino. She lives in Los Angeles, California and started her career in vfx on such films as *Titanic* before moving into the art department.

LORI AGOSTINO

Art Director

IMDB - R.I.P.D., The Butler, The Crazy Ones, Get Him to the Greek, Chicago Med

Q: Lori, would you tell me what you're doing these days?

A: Currently, I am working as production designer for *Chicago Med*, but I started as an Art director in both tv and film, which is how most production designer's start. When I worked on *The Butler* for example, I was the art director.

An art director specifically works for the films' designer to make sure that we bring all designs to fruition. This entails overseeing the construction of the sets; working closely with the construction coordinator, set designer and crew of the art department. We are responsible for running all aspects of the art department, which also includes graphics for signage, keeping on budget, and a timeline that will deliver a set to production on schedu

le. It is the art director's responsibility to make sure that all of these elements run smoothly

Q: At what point in Preproduction do you get involved?

A: I usually start a couple weeks after the production designer has been brought on, although with the changing landscape of the film/tv industry due to the economy, that timeframe has been compressed. For example, a construction coordinator normally would typically start a couple weeks after an art director but today they start almost at the same time, which creates an expectation of set construction starting earlier than it has in the past.

Q: Tell me about your role and crossover responsibility?

A: Our first responsibility is to the production designer so that they can spend their time designing which requires many different hats at different moments. When we start up preproduction, we first work from concepts to make sure that we can actually build the required sets and stay on budget. Once this is established, (and approved) we have the set designer draw up construction documents to build from.

At that point the focus is all about the particular set we are building. The art director will collect many different materials and have a show and tell with the production designer and construction coordinator to make sure that they will work.

As all of this is happening, we have our day-to-day work and meetings that we attend with production so that everyone is aware of where we are at, both budgetary and schedule wise. We are also the communicator of the dept. and disseminate information to other departments including, but not limited to grip, electric and set decoration, which all have their work revolve around our set in the preproduction phase.

Q: What are the 'must haves' for an Art Director?

A: A good art director must understand construction and why we build a set the way that we do. We read the script and follow the action of the character and make sure that a set is built in a way that gives correct access to production and this is no simple task. We have to understand which walls need to be built to wild (a wild wall is one that can be removed to give access to the camera for a particular shot).

You must have an understanding of film making to understand what type of shot is being framed and how they (production) need to move within the set's design. We are making sets to be filmed ultimately and if we deliver a set that causes problems for production, then we haven't done our job, no matter how beautiful the set is!

Q: Do you work as a sub-contractor, or as an employee for a Production Company?

A: I am a member of the art director's guild, IATSE Local 800. I am hired directly by a production designer to work for a production Company, which in turn works for a studio.

Q: Are your rates and compensation set by a guild?

A: We have a negotiated rate that is set by the ADG, and then we individually negotiate with the unit production manager to get paid above and beyond that scale rate. Each production is different for what they will pay for the position.

Q: What's the most challenging part of your job?

A: The hours, the changes, the current economy of cutting into Preproduction, while still having the same expectations to deliver without the budget.

Q: Have you ever mentored someone?

A: I love to have interns and mentor new crew. I think it is satisfying to see the excitement in their eyes, to watch them grow, and see how much fun we have doing a job we love.

Q: Best advice for an aspiring Art director?

A: You really have to make sure that this is what you want to do because, sometimes you're on location away from family and loved ones for long stints of time. The hours are long, the stress is high, and the expectations from production are many, but at the end of the day, if it's what you love doing, it's well worth it!

Q: Closing thoughts?

A: I'd just like to add that there is much satisfaction in being an art director. There is nothing like seeing your work on screen and realizing that others are sharing in the ride of the story because you helped to tell it!

STORYBOARD ARTIST

My sister India and brother John are incredible artists. I, on the other hand was able to channel my artistic talent into music. This was lucky for me, and the rest of the world, because my talents don't lean towards drawing, painting or even hand writing for that matter.

Dedicating yourself to the art of storyboarding requires lots of discipline; you also need to be extremely prolific because much of the visual design of a film is in your hands - literally. The director relies on you to represent their vision to the rest of the crew, producers and other stakeholders.

One of the most talented and sought after Storyboard Artists working on major Hollywood motion pictures is Jim Cornish. Jim based in London, England has been creating memorable movies for over 20 years.

JIM CORNISH

Storyboard Artist

IMDB - Dark Knight, Skyfall, Gravity, 47 Ronin, Event Horizon and (4) Harry Potter films, In the Heart of the Sea, Spectre, Tarzan, Fantastic Beasts, Life, Star Wars

Q: Jim, please tell me about the life of a Storyboard Artist?

A: The job of a storyboard artist is to take a scene or sequence and generate a visual version of the action based on a brief from the director and input from various department heads, production designer, vfx, stunts etc. When this sequence is drawn, it can then be distributed to the various departments as a document for discussion.

Changes will then be made based on ideas and/or limitations that arise out of the planning process, resulting in a final draft which should, in theory anyway, resemble the sequence as it appears in the cut film.

A storyboard can also be used as a tool for budgeting (a producer will get an idea of what the director is intending from looking through the drawn sequence and then start to work out the costs based on what he sees). Art departments, construction and vfx will start to break down the script 'shot by shot' to get a clearer idea of just what any action sequence entails – it's easy to write "and the boat sinks" but when the film is *TITANIC* there's often a lot more to it than meets the eye!!

Q: Are you part of a team?

A: Storyboard artists tend to work alone – or at least by themselves and we each have our own styles and methods of working. If there is more than one artist working on a feature then we will typically have our own sequences to draw and although we may discuss story plots and bounce ideas around we tend to get on with our own tasks and leave others to theirs.

On big budget effects-heavy films the number of artists will increase – on the *Harry Potter* films there could be as many as four artists servicing the production – owing to its high count of action and visual effects sequences. This brings with it its own problems because it starts to get difficult for the director to pass on enough information to maintain the workflow.

Q: How do you receive input from the director?

A: Each artist will get his or her brief from the director – it might be based on an hour long detailed conversation or be as fleeting as a passing word in an editing suite, or possibly even notes on a piece of paper. From that and the script it all comes down to the artists interpretation - and that's where the job differs depending on the artist and their style. The quicker you can get inside the directors head and get a feeling for what his approach to the film will be, the better you can interpret those ideas and embellish them with some of your own.

Q: Are there different types of storyboarding for creative presentation vs. production boards?

A: It largely comes down to the degree of finish and the length of time you have to do the job. Commercial boards tend to have a quicker turn around and might therefore be less finished - that is unless they are required to sell the concept to the client in which case they may well be full color panels that are highly rendered.

Film storyboards tend to go through several phases – they might be roughs, pasted together for discussion before being amended, they might be in thumbnail form so they can be passed on to a writer whilst being used for script development, or as the finished article for distribution throughout the shooting unit as a road map for the crew.

The storyboards for the film *Dark Knight* were very rough as they were drawn quite quickly to get an overall feel for the sequences rather than laboring over them and not covering all of the script points. The intention was to go back and "polish" them once they had been approved but the director, Chris Nolan, was happy that they covered the salient points and wanted to move on rather than commit valuable time to something that might change anyway come the day of shooting.

Q: Do you work with the director and producer?

A: I am the director's pencil monkey – I work for him first and foremost. The producer might tell the director he can't have something that I've drawn, because of cost or scheduling issues but it's the director that I answer to.

Q: I assume that you use specialized software in your job; did you have formal training?

A: My training stems from art collage and was done at a time when computers weren't so widespread, anything I've learned regarding computers is all self taught.

In days gone by it was done with nothing more than a pencil, pen or marker - hours of sitting with a pad of paper and the radio for company. Things have changed over the years and computers are more in evidence but it still tends to be a case of drawing on them rather than using specific software to create the panels.

I tend to use a Cintiq graphics tablet, which enables me to draw digitally - then any images are laid out using Photoshop and this allows them to be presented in a multitude of ways.

Q: How are storyboard artists paid, Jim?

A: If I work on a commercial I will get a daily rate or a rate per frame - if I work on a film it will be a weekly rate - contracts vary in length but are almost always done with the understanding that you will receive one weeks notice, so there is a degree of uncertainty attached to any and all work.

Q: Jim, photographers typically maintain ownership of the art they produce, how does this work for storyboard artists?

A: Well my biggest bugbear is the ownership of my images! While I am in the employ of a film production company any mark I might make on a piece of paper or screen, any drawing or design is immediately their property. This means I can't use those images to promote myself without their permission and certainly couldn't sell any of the work I produce afterwards – as an artist this is somewhat frustrating!

Q: Favorite project?

A: Working on *Batman Begins* was a ball - I was drawing Batman, what's not to enjoy about that? And, I was working with a storyboarding hero of mine, Martin Asbury. I was in awe of the man and always wanted to be a storyboard artist after seeing his work for *Alien 3;* now here I was sharing an office with him and we got on like a house on fire, I've never laughed so much whilst trying to hold a pen and I've never learned so much in six months as I did then.

Then there were the *Harry Potter* films. They were so big with so many people involved – from 2005 to 2010 I had a whole new family. We saw children being born, birthday parties, shared Christmas and sadly watched, as some much loved colleagues left us. It really was such a privilege to work with so many gifted, friendly and fun people for so long.

Q: Hardest part of your job?

A: Getting it right! You are only as good as your last drawing and the pressure is always on to get the director's vision down correctly. This is something that is often difficult to do because art like all creativity is so subjective and you seldom please all the people all the time. There are so many differing constraints so trying to juggle the needs and wants of various departments makes for a tricky life sometimes.

Q: What is a typical day at the office for you?

A: If I'm working in a film studio my day starts around 5:30 am; I'm an early riser and prefer to get a good start on the day. I will typically be at the drawing board by 7:00 am and if I've got my groove on and don't have any meetings to attend, my aim will be to keep going uninterrupted until lunch beckons at somewhere around 1pm.

More often than not I will grab a sandwich and be back at the board after a quick walk at around 1:30 pm and will crack on until 6:00 or 7:00 pm, by which time my eyes are normally out on stalks and my fingers have formed into a permanent claw. The day is done!

Q: It sounds like you get a lot of drawing in each day – how many frames?

A: In terms of frames per day it really depends on my day. If it's quiet and I'm left to get on with the job at hand I like to get 40 panels done, but if my day is punctuated by meetings and other commitments obviously the time spent drawing goes down and so too does the frame count. When it's needed I can bang out 80 frames in a day but as with most things the compromise is quality; you can have rough and quick, or slower and better. It's as simple as that; the things still need to be drawn, they don't just drop out of the end of my pencil!

Q. Do you work directly with talent?

A: You do meet actors on occasion (Sean Connery, Angelina Jolie, Daniel Radcliffe, Minnie Driver) but you don't really socialize with them. When at work they are working too so I am respectful of their space. When working on the *Harry Potter* films we regularly had celebrities visiting so might be in your office drawing away and suddenly Sarah Jessica Parker would be standing there, or Katie Melua would be standing behind you. I would smile and talk them through the process so they could understand what it is that we do… a small cog in a very big machine.

Q: Anything else you would like us to know about the job of a storyboard artist?

A: It sounds silly to say this but you've got to be able to draw. So often I see portfolios from students and the basics just aren't there. Once you have the basics down you can start learning about the job, handling the pressure, the various characters, politics, and the technical issues. The difficulty is, at the end of the day, as the name suggests, you're an artist, drawing, mark making, creating an image is fundamental to the job and it's where it starts and finishes.

When everything else is put to one side, I get paid well for doing something that I love and enjoy; I get pleasure from my job, from thinking about it, planning it and from executing it. I'm very critical of my work and prefer others to mine but I relish the chance to be part of the creative process and will never want to stop helping to find the best way to tell the story

CINEMATOGRAPHY

What's the first thing you notice while sitting in a theater after the introductory credits are complete, and the film starts? I believe the most exciting thing is the unveiling of a new world, a place I may have not seen before or a sideways view of something I see everyday.

It's the job of the Director of Cinematography, or DP to capture and deliver this vision. Working closely with the film's director and in cooperation with the production designer, and art director the DP creates a 'look' for the film. It is a complex process that incorporates storyboards, color testing, years of experience, and consulting with multiple other members of the film crew.

In recent years, the job of DP is also becoming reliant on technology so they must be willing to engage in the 'continuous learning' process which so many of us avoid. CGI and the enormous number of sfx in just about every film made today have to be taken into account and added to the skill set of anyone wanting to be a director of photography.

In my humble opinion, which I share so liberally, the DP is the 'magic' in filmmaking and I'm in awe of the work these people do. I was lucky enough to have two of the film industry's top DP's take the time to talk with me about their job and share their thoughts.

For me personally, the '300' movie franchises were some of the most visually satisfying films from the perspective of style that I have seen in many years. Simon Duggan, based in Australia shot the most recent installment *300: Rise of the Empire.*

SIMON DUGGAN

Director of Photography

IMDB - The Great Gatsby, I Robot, 300: Rise of the Empire, Warcraft, Hacksaw Ridge,
Isn't it Romantic

Q: Simon, I'm honored to ask you a few questions; let's start with a brief description of what you do?

A: As a director of photography I help create the look and feel of the film in collaboration with the director and the production designer. Through the early stages of pre production I make decisions on key crew such as the camera operators, camera assistants, gaffer and grip as well as much of the equipment required for the film.

During filming I work closely with the director, operators, grips, gaffer, camera assistants, makeup, hair, standby props, special fx, visual fx and many others to capture the films vision. Finally, when the film has been edited I become involved in postproduction and the final color grading and finishing of the film.

Recently on the film *300: Rise of an Empire* the producers took the film to Sofia, Bulgaria. Along with the local crew I sourced many key technicians from around the world to execute a very technically challenging film. We employed a multicultural crew with technicians from USA, Canada, England, Ireland, Australia, New Zealand, South Africa, Romania, Germany and Italy.

The film had literally thousands of visual effects shots, which required special backgrounds with almost every scene being shot against 'greenscreen', so preproduction was mainly focused on pre visualizing the environments and backgrounds for all the sequences to play out against.

On the stages the production designer built sets and landscapes for the actors so they were performing within real environments. The 'greenscreens' were behind the sets to extend the final image and give additional scale to what we were limited to on a film stage.

These days the director of photography also needs a deep knowledge of the visual effects process and works very closely with the vfx director and his team.

Due to the amount of computer generated imagery it was decided that *300* have a 'Post/Digital' 3D treatment applied to it rather than filming with stereo cameras. Having just had the previous experience of shooting the *Great Gatsby* in native Stereo 3D it really helped all my choices towards making *300* a good 3D film even though we were shooting single camera.

Choices such as lenses, camera movement and placement of midground and foreground elements along with understanding technically and aesthetically that when the images are finally projected in stereo, they will be convincing to the audience. As you can see the job of the DP is not as simple as one might suspect!

Q: Is there a difference between the title of Director of Photography and Cinematographer?

A: They basically mean the same although director of photography is a term that encompasses all the duties of the cinematographer, while on it's own refers more to the profession of cinematography.

Q: At what point are you brought in to the filmmaking process?

A: Normally I get involved early in preproduction depending on the complexity of the project. For example, I would be hired early in the process if the film had a lot of computer-generated imagery, or for logistical reasons such as defining the shooting budget and working with the location scout.

Q: What was your career path to becoming a DP?

A: I started my career as a camera trainee working for a fully crewed and equipped film production company specializing in tv commercials. I then worked my way up through the camera ranks and became a director of photography in my mid 20's.

As a DP I ventured out into the freelance world and was exposed to working with many directors, one of them being Alex Proyas who eventually gave me my 'big break' on my first major US film *I Robot* filmed in Canada.

Q: I understand this might be a hard question to answer but are you typically hired for your style, past experience in a genre, technical experience, relationships, or geographic location; or is it because you're just damn good at what you do?

A: The decision for a director to hire me often comes on the tail of my last film and word of mouth. I do however have a history of shooting action dramas with heavy CGI requirements that prove my technical and creative experience. Geographic location has never really entered into the equation except for my first smaller budget films that were filmed in my home city of Sydney, Australia.

Q: Is there a pay scale for a DP that rises with increased responsibility, or a standard fee paid as a percentage of the films budget? Residuals?

A: Remuneration is based on the experience of the DP and the demands of each film project The producers of a $100 million dollar film are always going to try to guarantee the right DP for the director and balance the demands of the production and adjust his pay rate accordingly. On a smaller independent film they may be only able to afford a certain fixed rate. This is often an opportunity for a talented DP with fewer credits, or in some cases a very experienced DP might decide to take on a project at a lower rate because it looks creatively rewarding.

Unfortunately DPs missed the residual payments boat, only writers, director's, actors, assistant directors and stunt crew get residuals.

Q: What was the most challenging film you've worked on, in terms of creating 'The Look' the director wanted?

A: The most challenging films are normally the first large scale films that a DP takes on and in this case it was *I Robot*. This film involved very complex computer generated imagery set in a futuristic world.

Every film has it's own creative challenge and it is mostly about establishing the envisioned "look" and maintaining it throughout the production so that the film has visual continuity. I believe that experience is probably the only way to remove the 'scare factor' in filmmaking.

Q: What might be the best steps or decisions I could make out of school that would give me a better chance of a career as a DP?

A: Film schools are great to get an introduction into the industry. I would try to get as much work experience as possible on film sets in any capacity you can find a way to get real 'on-set' experience and the chance to meet and talk with crew and potential future employers.

It's harder these days to get this on-set experience because of liability issues but if you can become a student member of a camera society they will often cover such costs as liability insurance.

Q: Tell me a story about a time when a director put you in the hot seat?

A: I really haven't had a situation where creatively I couldn't work out a seemingly impossible shot with a director although there have been some challenging times when I've spent hours prelighting a scene and then the director arrives with a new concept.

I have however literally been in the hot seat hanging out of a helicopter, operating a camera side mount where I felt lucky to get out alive. I was filming aerials around the mouth of the active volcano 'Mount Bromo' in Indonesia, flying through beautiful backlit clouds of what we later found out was volcanic ash that could have starved the engines of oxygen at any moment and sent us plummeting into the mouth of the volcano.

There was also another harrowing shoot in the Andes, South America when we were flying in a Bell helicopter fully loaded at maximum altitude of 12,000 ft. with me dangling out attached to a heavy camera side mount. We filmed some beautiful shots at the summit but by the time we headed back there was a heavy downdraft. All the pilot could do was fly at full power directly down the mountain with the downdraft to prevent us from being driven into the side of the mountain which was just feet away. It's those experiences that get the adrenaline pumping; fortunately we now use remote aerial camera heads!

Q: Was there a time when you asked your Gaffer to do the impossible?

A: It's often when you have a huge location at night or a large set on stage that creates an enormous logistical challenge for the gaffer. Then it becomes an expensive exercise in scale and the amount of lighting required to light a particular area and one, which the gaffer ends up going to great lengths to explain to the producer why it is costing so much.

I recently had to light a forest scene the size of a football field. The director's brief was that he wanted the forest to be lit with hot sunlight with parallel shafts of light as though as it had come from a million miles away. We only had a 35' ceiling so I asked my gaffer and crew to install thousands of spotlights mounted together in parallel in a row along the entire length of the 250' stage. It was an enormous time consuming, rigging and cabling exercise. The result was exactly as envisioned and the expense totally justified.

Q: What are your thoughts regarding the current movement towards filmmakers producing and releasing indie films via the web and bypassing the large studios altogether?

A: I think it's great that filmmaking is so accessible now and indie films can be shot on a SLR and find their release on the web, however as long as the studios can make a profit and attract the audiences there will always be a market for the large budget films.

Q: What's the best time you have ever had working on a film?

A: I would have to say the high profile films *I Robot, Die Hard 4, The Great Gatsby* and more recently *Warcraft* currently in postproduction have been my favorites. Every image was a challenge yet fun to create and we had a wonderful cast and crew who made all those films such a personally enjoyable experience.

Q: Have you ever had an intern?

A: On the *Great Gatsby* we set up a work experience program through the Australian cinematographers Society where we took on several student members one at a time for a period of 2 weeks. They all loved the opportunity to be a part of the process and learned an incredible amount in a very short time span.

Q: Is the job of a world class DP a viable long-term career in the future?

A: It is a rapidly changing world in the film industry but there will always be the need for a DP in some capacity. The structure of what we as DPs have been doing for the last few decades has gradually changed and in just the last few years we've seen radical changes with so many new affordable digital image capture options and the diversification of media such as the internet and cable.

Stuart Dryburgh was one of the very first people to step forward and offer to take my questions. He is a Cinematographer, Director of Photography or in France Stuart is the Chief Operator; in Germany he is the Fotograf, and in England sometimes he is called the Lighting Cameraman. Whatever you call him he is the person that captures the magnificent images you see on the big screen! With close to 50 feature film credits Stuart is in an elite group.

Stuart Dryburgh - Photo Courtesy of Wilson Webb

STUART DRYBURGH
Director of Photography

IMDB - Secret life of Walter Mitty, The Piano, Alice Through the Looking Glass, The Great Wall, Gifted, The Upside

Q: Stuart, would you describe what you do?

A: The Director of Photography is the person on a film crew who is primarily in command of the camera department, and responsible for the composition of shots, camera movement, lighting and exposure.

He or she will also work closely with the director, producers and production design team to coordinate the look of the production and the general storytelling as it relates to the camera. The degree that they are responsible for specific camera placement and lensing choices will depend on the director. Some, like Michael Mann, will want to make most if not all of those decisions while others like Ben Stiller will take a more collaborative approach. Some directors will prefer to leave all of the camera and shot choices to the DP, focusing their energies on performance and the dialog.

The DP is also responsible for making sure the dailies (daily rush prints in days past) correctly represent his intentions. On a full film-to-film production, this involves communicating with the dailies print timer at the lab, and reviewing the print, usually in company with the director.

Q: Please tell us about your team - with whom do you work most closely and how do you interact with each other?

A: The key players on my team are the key grip and gaffer. The camera department can be as small as myself and one assistant, (really a documentary crew) or may include one or more camera operators, some of whom might be specialists; Steadicam operator, aerial, underwater or high speed camera car. Also, I would confer with any additional camera crews, 2nd unit, vfx or miniatures to make sure the movie is consistent in style.

The gaffer is my right arm when it comes to lighting - a good gaffer can execute precisely the lighting requests of the DP, and in my case as an ex gaffer myself these requests might be (annoyingly) specific as to how I want something rigged.

The relationship with the key grip depends on where you are: in Europe, Australasia or Asia, the grip is primarily responsible for rigging the camera, whether on a simple tripod, or on a camera vehicle, be it a car truck airplane or boat. They are also responsible for camera cranes and dollies, as well as all mechanical camera movement. A good camera grip will not only have a repertoire of off the shelf rigging solutions, but also the expertise to create rigs from scratch when required. In the US, the grip has additional duties including working closely with the gaffer.

Q: You travel extensively in your job, is this perk or necessary evil?

A: For me it is definitely a perk that lets me see way more of the world, and often experience the intimate details of people's lives in a way I could never experience as a tourist. However, when I do have a vacation, I will often choose to spend it at home with my family, or at nearby beaches or mountains.

Q: Did you major as a film student at some point?

A: I didn't have any formal film education, but I did complete a 5-year degree in Architecture at Auchland University in 1977. This was a great visual arts education, and definitely helps in 3 dimensional and spatial thinking. It also cultivated an ability to draw and communicate visually.

Q: You've worked on so many high profile projects, what's your typical process?

A: Getting hired usually starts with a phone call from my agent saying that so-and-so is interested in me for a project. I then read the script and decide if it is something I am interested in taking on. If so, a meeting is set with the director, and sometimes the producer (s). I usually try to bring some visual reference with me to this meeting and if they like me I'm hired on the film. This might be a helpful description of the process and what I might be doing.

Preproduction – Typically, for the DP on a feature film, this starts 6 to 10 weeks prior to the start of principle photography. Much of this time is taken up with meetings with the director to plan shots, visits to locations, consulting with other department heads especially art, costume and visual effects (vfx) and the recruitment my key crew members for the camera department. We might also shoot tests, which I like to do early on in preproduction, as well as still photographs to experiment with the 'look' of the film, and to help in choosing lenses, filters, and lighting techniques.

Production – Most shooting days commence with a 'blocking' rehearsal. The cast will run through the scene, which is watched by the director, DP and the script supervisor, and sometimes other key crew. Once the director is happy, he and the cast show the scene to the full crew, the cast goes of into hair and makeup, and the crew set about putting together the technical aspects of the scene, based on what they have just seen. Camera positions, dollies or cranes, lighting and special effects rigs are all finalized at this stage, and the DP along with the assistant director is very much in charge at this stage.

Often the director will leave the set while all this tech work takes place to meet with cast members or the writers, or to approve costume and makeup changes. Once the DP feels the set s ready to shoot, the cast and director return and shooting commences. This process is repeated to a greater or lesser degree for each camera set up throughout the day. The day ends after the crew wraps with review of the previous days 'dailies', either in a screening room with the director, or more frequently these days, viewing digital dailies on a computer or HD screen.

Postproduction – the DP does not typically get involved in editing the film, but near the end of that process is called in to supervise the final color and density or the release print or more commonly now called the DCP (digital cinema package). In a photochemical laboratory the DP consults with a color timer, who will then make a series of test prints, making adjustments each time to the DP's notes, until every one is happy and an answer print is struck.

In a digital finish, this 'grading' of the film takes place in a digital suite in a process known as Digital Intermediate (DI). Working with a DI colorist the DP adjusts the color and density and contrast of each scene until satisfied with the result. This then becomes the master reference for all film prints, DCPs and video masters for tv and DVD/Blue Ray release.

Q: What's the length of time you devote to a typical project?

A: Most feature projects are between 45-60 days shooting, independent films 20-40 days and tv pilot episodes 12- 20 days.

Q: Stuart, you work at the top of your field and I'm sure you are well compensated. Would you speak to long tail revenue?

A: For all sorts of complex political and historical reasons, neither the DP, nor any member of the camera department receives residuals or royalties. The exception would be on some low budget films, where the DP might reduce his compensation dramatically in exchange for a share in any future profit. This is referred to being given 'points' in the picture. As a result I still receive the occasional (very small) checks from some independent projects I've taken on.

Q: Tell me something that most people don't know about you?

A: That I trained to be an architect, and through friends who were working in the nascent New Zealand film industry in the late 1970s, got interested in being a film maker myself, and was hired because I was interested, unemployed, and therefore available. I then received some of the best on the job training you could imagine. A very fortunate and lucky piece of timing!

Q: Do you have a favorite film project?

A: I think it may have been *In My Fathers Den*, an independent New Zealand film made around 2003 by young kiwi writer director Brad McGann, now sadly deceased. An intimate family drama set in the rugged rural heartland of New Zealand's South Island, I worked very closely with Brad, a first time feature director, and his cast, operated the camera myself and felt more than ever that I was using the camera to tell a story the way a writer wields a pen or a painter a brush. It was an exceptionally satisfying creative experience, on a really terrific little film that has sadly been little seen in the US.

Q: Hardest part of your job?

A: The politics, managing expectations, and balancing the efficient use of time and resources against the creative requirements and desires of the films creative team.

Q: What was the funniest thing that ever happened on a set, during a shoot?

A: We were on the New Zealand production of *Once Were Warriors*, directed by Lee Tamahori when, the morning after we had thrown a party to 'christen' a large bar set, the only two people who made it to the studio at call time were myself and the director. The rest of the crew, and cast, drifted in over the next hour or so, mostly looking very unwell after an excellent party!

Q: What advice might you have for a young filmmaker?

A: Assuming they want to be a DP one day, there are two main routes that actually work. One, the traditional, union path, is to start at the bottom, often as a prep technician in a camera rental house, where they will meet many camera assistants, and eventually might be able to persuade one to take them on a film as a loader or camera PA. It is a long path but does work.

Less traditional, and riskier would be to just do it! Find some like-minded young filmmakers, in or out of a regular film school setting, and start making films together. If you are lucky enough to make one that is even moderately successful, you will be on the way to having a career. But it is all a crap shoot – there is a saying in the film industry, that, 'It is better to be lucky than talented!' – but, if you do get lucky, you'd better have the talent to take advantage of that luck.

CASTING

Most films require a cast and the person that finds and hires them is the Casting director! They need to have great connections, incredible insight into human nature and the ability to weed through thousands of potential candidates to find the perfect talent. A knowledgeable Casting director is essential to any film, because without the talent to fulfill the roles, the project has no chance of real financial or critical success.

Carl Proctor trained as an actor and worked in theater for several years before turning to casting as a career. He is considered one of London's busiest Casting directors and works primarily in film and tv. Recently, Carl was the Casting director on the mini-series *The Bible*.

CARL PROCTOR

Casting Director

IMDB - Shadow of the Vampire, The Bible, Breakdown, Lucid

Q: Carl, would you tell us about your job?

A: The role and influence of a casting director can vary significantly from one project to another but most often our job is to come up with casting ideas and a selection of Actors and then the director and producer will choose who they want to cast, with direct offers going to the better known actors.

Having read the script and got some idea of character descriptions, I would ideally then have a meeting with the director and sometimes the producer to get their thoughts on the types I am to look for but if the director is filming abroad and all I get is an 'English Brad Pitt' type, so be it.

The Bible mini-series was indeed a massive undertaking. I worked on this project, with a couple of assistants for eight months. There were also two people in Morocco who cast local actors in the very small speaking roles as well as the many extras.

Scripts were still being finalized after the shoot began so we were casting the later episodes well into the overall shoot period. With the exception of our Portuguese Jesus, British actors played the principal roles. The project was always going to be sold on its quality and subject matter so I was not under any pressure to secure very well known actors, just good and suitable ones. Consequently, we were able to cast the very best of the British acting talent base.

Q: What is the skill set of a successful Casting director?

A: For one reason or another, casting often starts closer to the shoot date than is ideal and it's not often a leisurely process so thriving under pressure is a very useful quality.

Number two would be a good memory or at least having a system that enables you to deliver enough good and interesting ideas for each role.

Q: For *The Bible* miniseries you cast Diogo Morgado as Jesus. Might you explain the process you went through to cast him in this role?

A: We auditioned a lot of British actors for this part. Some were very good and a couple came close, but Mark Burnett and Roma Downey had a very clear idea of what they were looking for and had set the bar very high. They knew how much focus there would be on this character and that they needed someone special, not just a good actor but also someone with huge charisma. They needed to have that X Factor.

So we quickly widened the search and found Diogo. He put himself on tape and then met Mark and Roma in LA. They loved him and knew immediately that he was their Jesus. Diogo was already doing pretty well in Portugal and was in the process of moving to LA so I think we got him at a good time. He was keen from the start but could have had no idea at the time that the series was going to be such a huge success and give him the exposure that it did and continued to do through the film *Son of God.*

Q: Do you work with the director, and producer?

A: Mostly, I interact with the director but often the producer as well, or sometimes exclusively the producer. Meetings are not always practical or necessary so I often email lists of suggestions to the director and producer; they will then discuss people with me and between themselves and offers will go out to the favorites.

In film, actors with 'value' are often needed to secure finance, so the producer will be heavily involved in the process of casting principal roles. In my experience, mainly working in film and television, the producer is often present and actively involved in the casting process alongside the director. I seem to have worked with a lot of producers who have directed or written and are as able as the director to make the right creative decisions.

Q: How are you hired?

A: Casting directors often don't have agents as a lot of our work comes directly to us. It might be handy sometimes to have someone to do a deal but agreements can be fairly simple and the fees are often not very negotiable. So in my experience it is mainly people recommending me to others or people that I have worked with before. Sometimes I might need to go in for an interview where I'm up against a few other casting directors, but more often than not, I just get a call offering me the job.

Q: How are Casting directors compensated?

A: The workload can vary massively from one project to another so in order for me to consider an offer I have to make a judgment up front about how big the job might be.

There are many factors to weigh because it isn't just number of parts but the types that have an impact on my workload. If it's three ordinary young couples, it could all be very quick and easy as there are a lot of them and they are more likely to be keen. But, if some of the characters require specific skills, unusual looks, particular accents, etc., it can take much longer.

Unrealistic expectations from a producer often lead to a lot of actors declining before someone finally accepts, but if the money is good there is more chance of securing first choices. All of this has an impact when trying to assess the likely workload and establish what might be an appropriate fee. Sometimes we might be paid a small fee at an early, speculative stage just to make suggestions and then receive the proper casting fee when the film is fully funded and green-lit.

Q: What role does technology play in your job?

A: Well the software application Spotlight makes our job much easier than in most other countries where a database or ability to do specific searches either doesn't exist or is limited It is now very easy to upload a casting or self taping to a remote site for selected people to view from anywhere in the world. We used ' another application Castit on *The Bible* series, which worked well when producers or directors were in LA or Morocco.

Q: Do you have a favorite project?

A: I think it was *probably Shadow of the Vampire*. We had John Malkovich and Willem Dafoe firmly attached so no more value was needed. I asked the Elias Merhige (director) if he wanted to see lots of people for the other roles or if I should just bring in a couple of very good actors for each part. He chose the latter so we spent just two days meeting actors, some of whom were friends of mine from RADA. It was Eddie Izzard's second acting job.

Q: What is the most challenging part of your job?

A: I think it is when expectations are unrealistic. It is always worth trying, but when you know it is highly unlikely that an 'A' lister is going to sign on for a low budget film with a first time director and the funding is conditional on having him/her, it's hard to be enthusiastic.

Q: What's your take on casting as a career path?

A: When I left RADA as an actor a long time ago, there seemed to be just a handful of casting directors in London. There are now a many of us and nowhere near enough work to keep everyone employed full-time. So I would say that casting these days is something to pursue only if you are very keen to do it. You could try to get a job (even as an intern initially) with a busy casting director (or an agent) and learn. Go to the theatre, watch tv, and film. Keep up with new talent; that type of thing.

Q: Last thoughts?

A: Casting can be very rewarding and fun. At the end of the day there is a finished product on the screen that you feel very much a part of creating and it's there for posterity. But…be prepared for long, hard days on occasion.

COSTUME DESIGNER

I've always been amazed at the subtle difference between what makes a believable Western and one that looks cheesy on screen. Of course, there are many factors including the budget, filming style, production design, the acting, and direction, but one of the most important parts of the puzzle is something more subtle; the costume design.

Think about it - most people in Westerns depict cowboys and frontiersmen of the early 1800's that only bathed during seasonal changes when the weather was mild and only changed clothes when they wore out! They didn't shave or cut their hair regularly and so on So when I see a Western with an actor wearing nice pressed jeans, a clean ten-gallon hat, and no dirt under his fingernails, it just doesn't feel all that authentic.

The costume designer's job is to help us suspend reality and draw us into a believable time, or place; it is their responsibility to design, fabricate, or acquire all of costumes the actresses and actors wear. They need to be well versed in many cultures, garments, history, be masters of research and let's not forget the differentiating characteristic that sets a successful and not so successful costume designer apart - a curious, creative mind.

One of my favorite series in recent past has been *True Blood*, not so much because of an affinity for vamps, but for the intriguing alternate *human* fantasy. The creator and writers effortlessly move us from place to place, and through time in an authentic way while always keeping us firmly seated in present southern Louisiana.

Audrey Fisher, costume designer was responsible for helping us believe the fantasy. Educated at Occidental College and NYU's Tisch School of the Arts, she is sought after because of her in-depth historic knowledge, creative eye, and attention to detail.

Photo Courtesy of Michele K. Short

AUDREY FISHER

Costume Designer

IMDB - True Blood, Milk, That 70's Show, The Man in the High Castle, Girlboss, Barry

Q: Audrey, there are many roles in the Costume Department including Designer, Costumer, Set Costumer, Costume Supervisor, etc.? Would you mind discussing yours and the hierarchy of the Costume department?

A: I'm the head of the costume department, and I am responsible for the design or "look" of every costume for every character in the script. I am closely partnered, however, by talented colleagues in the costume department who are both in the Costume Designers Guild Local 892, like myself, and our sister union, the Motion Picture Costumers Union Local 705.

My assistant costume designer, also in the guild, is my right hand and oversees all the detailed work that goes into creating the costumes, from script to screen. My costume supervisor, a member of Local 705, is the manager of the department, handling for instance hiring, budgeting, and paperwork; she interfaces with our producers daily to get what we need to get the job done.

My key costumer supervises the busy workflow in the costume department, and is also responsible for prepping the costumes, under my supervision, for the background actors in large crowd scenes.

My costume buyer shops all day, every day, for whatever we need to do costume fittings, as well as other departmental needs, like supplies for the sewing room.

My on-set costumers are the caretakers of the costumes once they leave the costume department and go to the wardrobe truck; they handle continuity, which is a big part of a bloody action episodic like *True Blood*, and they make sure the costume is worn according to my specifications for the duration of the time that costume is on camera. We also have production assistants in the department, and that is the only non-union position.

Q: Your work *True Blood* must have been incredibly rewarding and challenging at the same time. Would you talk a little bit about how you kept the design fresh and true to the story at the same time?

A: *True Blood* was a wonderful show to create costumes for because of the varied characters of each script: small-town Louisiana folk, glamorous vampires and then of course all kinds of characters in flashback scenes ranging from 3500 BC to Charles II's court of 1650 to the Civil War to San Francisco 1905 to Los Angeles 1930, and beyond!

The script is always my roadmap, and that's why the design stays exciting: the costumes supported the evolving narrative that the writers kept fresh for all 7 seasons.

Q: Where should I live if I want to be a Costume Designer, or does it matter?

A: To pursue costume design, I feel it's best to be in a city with a lot of production. If you are just starting out, and not yet in the union, that gives you more opportunity to design non-union projects, and one of those might get "flipped" or unionized. Also, you could meet the people who are working in union productions who might someday hire you.

My best advice is to always be a professional and dedicated worker, and carefully cultivate your relationships. The best way to get more design work is through colleagues who have noticed and appreciated your talent and work ethic.

Q: What is the normal path someone might take entering the world of costume design?

A: There are many paths to the same destination. Some go through a costume design program; some start in fashion; others have a life-long interest in clothing and design and start working towards the goal of creating costumes. The most important thing is a love of costume design, and that paired with talent, creativity and perseverance will guide you to success.

Q: What role did a formal education play in your career, if any?

A: Originally I wanted to be a dramaturg, and so to that end I pursued an MA in Performance Studies at NYU. While I was there my love of design merged with my theatre experience, and I started making costumes for productions with my grad school colleagues.

Now I consider myself a dramaturg of clothing for each production, because that is really what a costume designer is: an interpreter of the script into the language of clothing.

Q: What is the typical length of time you have to prepare and design for an episode of *True Blood*?

A: After our standard 4-week prep at the beginning of each season, and principal photography begins, we are always prepping while shooting simultaneously, so it's honestly hard to say.

Sometimes a scene gets pulled up and we have a half a day to figure it out; other times we know something is on the horizon and get an early start. But we can never prep too far ahead as scripts change; casting comes late or changes; and important meetings with decision-makers only happen close to the time that each new episode starts. I'd say the least amount of time I have had to prep is 12 hours; the most is 3 weeks.

Q: At the level you work, you are well compensated. Please explain how people in the Costume Department are paid?

A: Costume designers are paid a flat rate for each week of work. As creative department heads we are considered on-call employees. I am not paid for overtime hours.

My assistant costume designer has the same deal, which is a tough break as ACDs often work the longest hours, and are not compensated for all that time as their 705 colleagues are. Of course ACDs are on track to be designers, so hopefully all that hard work pays off, but still it requires a lot of energy and stamina.

Local 705 costumers are paid hourly, and do receive overtime payment. This distinction sometimes guides the prospective designer or costumer in the way he or she enters the business.

My weekly rate varies from production to production, but one hopes to maintain a baseline and grow from that amount. I have an agent who helps to negotiate my fee on each show, and it's *always* a negotiation.

Q: What is the most challenging part of your job?

A: Creative problem solving on a tight deadline and budget. Also, making decisions quickly so work can progress. Both are equally important to the costume design process proceeding smoothly.

Q: What was the funniest thing that's ever happened on a set, during a shoot?

A: By far the funniest (in retrospect only!) is one shoot day when everyone on my team including me managed to miss the fact that an actress was in the scene that was about to shoot and without a costume; as she walked up to her trailer, my key costumer all of a sudden realized our oversight, and calmly called my cell as I rode to set and announced: "Holly is in the scene." I vaulted out of the van and ran into Macy's, which was thankfully adjacent to our base camp and within 15 minutes had fit the actress in a great looking costume. Happily the scene didn't call for a ball gown; it was pajamas…so I could pull it off. It always works out!

Q: What are the most important traits of a successful of Costume Designer?

The 5 Cs:

    1. Confidence
    2. Clarity
    3. Creativity
    4. Communication
    5. Commitment

Q: What advice might you give a young person wanting to be a Costume Designer?

A: My best advice is to reach out to costume designers that are inspirational. Research their projects, study their design choices, and try to visualize their process. Then reach out! I got several of my first theatrical assistant designer gigs by writing letters to designers I admired. I was respectful and deferential, and communicated what I loved about the design, and how honored I would be to learn from the designer.

Those hand-written letters got me interviews, and at least one lead to an amazing job. Sounds old fashioned, I know, and maybe in today's world email is standard. But there is something profound and intimate about a well-written letter.

The take-away really should be: find designers who inspire, and learn from them.

And then my second piece of advice would be to say yes to as many design jobs as possible to meet people and make as many connections as possible, always do your very best in everything you do, treat everyone around you with respect from the background actors to the caterer to the teamsters to the director to the actor to the producers.

It takes a village, and you need to respect all your colleagues equally. Finally, this Dale Carnegie quote sums it up for me: "Flaming enthusiasm, backed up by horse sense and persistence, is the quality that most frequently makes for success."

Q: Have you ever mentored someone or had an intern?

A: HBO has a very strict policy regarding interns, so I have had the pleasure of having only one Academy of Motion Picture Arts and Sciences intern during my tenure. I look forward to having interns in the future, and helping to mentor young designers, because I think it's a great way to keep the craft of costume design strong and vibrant by helping an energetic young designer learn the ropes!

LINE PRODUCER

I, like you, am sometimes confused by crew titles, so when I approach an area that needs a little extra explanation, I'll slow down and do my best to clue you in. I believe this to be the case with the 'line producer' and the 'unit production manager'.

The **'Line Producer'** is the person that creates the budgets for a production and is responsible for them throughout the course of a production.

The UPM or **'Unit Production Manager'** is tasked with executing the 'line producer's' plan and budget and reporting back.

In many countries, the line producer in particular is an often-misunderstood job title, because the line producer, unit production manager, unit manager, and production supervisor all do the same exact job. There are however, small distinctions.

Leifur Dagfinnsson is chairman and founding partner of Iceland based *TRUENORTH*, a production company whose many credits include blockbusters like *Thor, Walter Mitty, and Flags of our Fathers*; films that required incredibly dramatic locations like the ones that only Iceland can offer.

Leifur Dagfinnsson (left) with Matt Damon

LEIFUR B.DAGFINNSSON

Line Producer

IMDB - Thor, Oblivion, The Fifth Estate, The Journey Home, Star Wars, The Journey

Home

Q: Leifur, thank you for sharing your thoughts about the film industry in Iceland, and in particular the role of a Line Producer.

A: Well thank you Michael. My role as a line producer is basically running the actual production, making sure we have the right size crew, putting the right team together, schedule and budgeting production.

When filming in Iceland and especially on larger international films the tendency is to film in fairly remote locations, which can be challenging for film crews; for example on the Tom Cruise's *Oblivion* we filmed on a top of a mountain, only accessible by helicopters so another role I take is considering the location logistics.

Q: What is the difference between the title of 'UPM' and 'line producer'?

A: In my opinion they are one in the same and I'm not sure how or when this changed. LP's or UPM's run the day to day business of the production, schedule, budget, and then report to the producer who is in direct dialogue with the director and main cast members.

Q: You run 'TRUENORTH', one of the leading production companies in Iceland and work with today's top directors. What has been the most challenging film to date for your company?

A: I would have to say Clint Eastwood's *Flags of Our Fathers*, where the main challenge was to recreate a battle set in the Pacific during WW2. It was probably the only contemporary war ever held in Iceland since the Viking era! The size of the crew was over 500 and there were an additional 500 extras. We filmed for 5 weeks on the coastline at the southwestern tip of Iceland and everything ran very smoothly, due to good preparation on our part and the great team Clint brought along.

Q: How are Line producers paid? Is it salaried or by the project, and would I be able to make a good living assuming I have the drive, and talent to get the job done?

A: Salary is normally based on the project and depending on the size of the film's budget and yes one can make a very good living.

Q: I would imagine that the best line producers are trained or mentored?

A: Yes, we have mentored some of our current staff – which has become a very enjoyable experience for us. It gives me great pleasure to see them flourish and turn out to be great production managers - and soon to be Line producers.

Q: What types of things might Leifur B. Dagfinnsson be doing on any given day?

A: That all depends whether we are in production or not. Day to day running the company takes most of my time, which involves pitching locations or budgeting for films that wish to shoot in Iceland.

My days are different when in production; I normally start the day on location to make sure everything is running smoothly then go into production office and sign paperwork and make sure we are on schedule and budget for the next filming day. There's a lot more to my day than this but it might be a bit too much for your book Michael!

Q: If I were interested in a career as a line producer and just out of college, or trade school, what advice might you give me?

A: Get a job as a PA in production, location or the ADs department. ADs and location managers often tend to become line producers – as these jobs bring many of the elements & skills together that are required to become successful line producer.

Q: What was most enjoyable part of your job?

A: Collaboration, the people I meet and work with, the creative challenges, and that there is always a new and different task or problem to solve!

Q: Given that you live in Iceland, how important is geographic location in your business?

A: There are pros and cons, but with todays technology and accessible travel options Iceland is not that remote - but then again most of the films I´ve been involved with have been filmed in Iceland.

UNIT PRODUCTION MANAGER

"I need 15 more people today to get this 10 story building to look the way you want to see it Mr. DP, otherwise it just can't be built on time!" This statement cuts to the heart of the unit production manager, the person responsible for seeing that a film comes in on-time and on-budget; at least through principle photography. They have to say "No" a lot.

Mark Kamine started in the business as a location assistant and quickly moved to location manager on such projects as *The Sopranos* and *Men in Black* before jumping to the unit production manager role. Many films have benefitted from Mark's skill set, most recently *Silver Linings Playbook, 42,* and *American Hustle*. I should also mention that he is a well-respected producer in his own right and on a trajectory to become an award winning executive producer.

MARK KAMINE
Unit Production Manager
IMDB - Ted, The Fighter, Shutter Island, A Million Ways to Die in the West, Ted 2, Bad Moms

Q: Mark, would you tell me what the UPM is responsible for and maybe use *Silver Linings Playbook* as an example?

A: The UPM makes sure everything is getting done as efficiently as possible and in a timely manner. It can start as early as renting office space, though sometimes a line producer will get that started. So it includes hiring crew, making deals with them, making deals for equipment and trucks. You also check all department budgets initially and keep track of how they're doing as the money starts getting spent.

Some examples from *Silver Linings*: I went with the line producer to meetings with the 'Eagles' when we were hoping for NFL cooperation (the bookie aspect of the Robert DeNiro character didn't meet NFL standards in a script, so we did the movie without using things like player likenesses and real footage).

Also, we had a bunch of meetings and discussions with the art and location departments about using existing dance studios in Philly. David O. Russell prefers to shoot in real locations, not on stages, whenever possible, but that turned out not to be practical, schedule-wise, so we built the rehearsal studio.

Q: How does the role of UPM differ from a production supervisor, or are they the same job with different titles?

A: They are sometimes the same job. Sometimes it's a union distinction. Sometimes the UPM works with a production supervisor under her/him, the supervisor helping with the workload because part of a UPM's job is approving more or less everything including all purchases, rentals, check requests, petty cash, bills from the camera house, the caterer, and the hotel where the crew or actors are staying.

On *42* we had a supervisor, Noelle Green, who helped a ton. We were in 3 different states prepping, shooting or wrapping at the same time and had grip, electric and construction crews all over the place. We divided up the departments and dealt with the film in that way.

Q: Tell me a bit about the hierarchy of the crew. As the UPM you are at the top of the food chain and hold the title of 'boss' in many respects; who answers to whom under you?

A: You're only a boss in a manner of speaking in that you are watching the money closely and thus what everyone is doing with it. As UPM I feel perfectly free to question anyone about what they're doing, whether it's building sets, requesting camera, lighting and grip rentals, buying food, or wanting to hire additional workers. You have to say "No" to a lot of requests.

The production designer or the director of photography don't consider the UPM her/his boss and probably think of that person as more of a hindrance. But you have to be willing to say "No." I've even (in the most delicate way possible) had to tell directors they need to finish a scene by a certain time, or camera wrap by a certain hour of the day, or break for lunch maybe when they'd rather just keep shooting. Not fun, but a necessity.

Q: Mark, what drew you into the film business?

A: I love movies. You can make good money, and be part of something that is creative. It's alternately both exhausting and fulfilling. I've gotten pretty used to the intense periods of work followed by bouts of unemployment (usually about 1 month longer than I would like, but that's freelance work for you).

Q: Is there a logical path to the role of UPM, and would it be a sustainable career option for the right person?

A: People definitely make careers out of this job and you can make a nice living. There are also lots of ways in. You can work your way up in the office, as an accountant, in locations as I did (a lot of New York people do this), or as an Assistant director.

Q: Mark, what project has been the most fun and enjoyable for you to work on?

A: Well I must say I had a great time on the Paris segment of *The Sopranos*. The scouting, and then the shoot were tons of fun. We had a wonderful director, Tim Van Patten, a great 1ST AD, Michael DeCasper, and a French crew that had done lots of bits and pieces of movies and tv shows with a slightly different approach to the job that was interesting to see.

Q: Are UPM's unionized and would you speak to compensation?

A: UPM's are normally in the Director's Guild of America (DGA) – as long as the director is in the Guild, you have to have a DGA UPM. Normally your salary is weekly, with minimums (called scale in the film biz) and set by the DGA, though you can get above-scale rates based on experience and precedent. With non-DGA directors (usually first time or low budget directors), you're on your own, though different budget levels come with pretty standard salary expectations for this position.

Once again I thought a few words from Olivier Arnesen who spoke earlier about the role of a producer might be helpful. He worked his way up through the ranks and experienced many production related jobs including that of Production Manager.

OLIVIER ARNESEN
Production Manager

IMDB – Pirates of the Caribbean, Body of Lies, National Treasure, Ballers

Q: Olivier, what drew you into the film business? What is the magic for you?

A: The big screen always captivated me and even though I started on projects that were small and not for episodic or film the idea of sewing together someone's imagination through cameras, sound, editing was just as magical as what I would see in the movies; those were my draws.

Q: Can you outline a typical day for you as a Production Manager once principle-shooting starts?

A: I am not on set but work from the office. My day consists of the following:
- Looking at the preliminary call sheet drawn up by the 1st and 2nd AD's to review what the following day calls for and then I make sure we have all the necessary specialty gear, or personnel we will require.

- I interface with camera, grip, and lighting and make sure that gear wise I am addressing any requests of additional equipment outside the scope of what we typically carry for the run of the show.

- During the course of filming I am engaged in the day-to-day operations of running production.

Q: Olivier, you and I worked together for a long time and I know just how dedicated and good you are at your job. How do you find work and market yourself?

A: In my case it is primarily by word of mouth; I find work through the people I have worked for. I've also used what is commonly know as the 'Production Weekly' that lists all production taking place in and out of the states.

Q: Where would you like your career to go from here?

A: I see myself moving from the logistics and more so to the creative side and hope to produce my own ideas for either tv/film.

Q: I saw that you are Co-producer on the hit tv series _Ballers_ starring 'The Rock'.

A: Yes that is correct. It is a great show in every respect, and I'm proud to be part of such a successful production where I get to work with an amazing crew.

Q: Olivier, do you have a project that stands out as a favorite?

A: Yes, I have 2. I worked on _Body of Lies_ with Ridley Scott and _Déjà vu_ with Tony Scott. Working with both the Scott Brothers (Ridley and Tony) was such a terrific experience both professionally and personally. I learned so much.

VISUAL FX

We now move from practical filming and production to the unreal world of Visual FX production. Today virtually every major film produced has some degree of visual computer generated imagery.

I remember when I first saw *The Matrix* I was astounded by the way they could stop the action and move in slow motion around them. My coworkers and I talked about it every day at our production company every one of our clients wanted that effect woven into their productions.

Vince Cirelli is Vice President and VFX Supervisor at 'Luma Pictures', a Visual Effects company co-located in both Los Angeles, and Melbourne, Australia. I would be correct in saying that Vince has worked on most of the blockbuster films of the past decade.

VINCE CIRELLI

Visual Effects Supervisor

IMDB - The Avengers, Guardian of the Galaxy, Ironman 3, Ant-Man, Avengers: Age of Ultron, In the Heart of the Sea, Deadpool, Captain America, Dr. Strange, The Accountant, Black Panther, Thor

Q: Vince, thank you for taking the time to share your thoughts. What does a VFX Supervisor do for a film?

A: Well, I'm the Vice President of Luma Pictures, and also the senior vfx supervisor. My executive duties include global planning, company strategies, development, artist management, technology research, PR, and most importantly the day-to-day operation of all things production.

Being the creative and technical liaison to all client side producers, supervisors, and directors, I guide Luma's Los Angeles and Melbourne international teams through complex character, creature effects and final shot design.

Q: What's the main difference between working as a sfx specialist for a feature film and what you did in your advertising agency days?

A: I would say that the feature work I do now is focused more around very complex CG design, integrating photo real creatures, digital humans, and architecture into filmed plates.

Prior to my film work, I spent a lot of time as a creative director buried in design work centered on illustration, branding, and new media. It was very rewarding, in that branding and marketing can be thrilling because not only does it include a visual component, but you're also helping to conceptually sculpt the publics perception of any given property or company.

However, nowadays I get to go home and tell my daughter about the vast worlds and characters we create which don't actually exist outside of the computer, which for me is a hell of a lot more fun.

Q: What would you consider the most important skills for someone in the vfx arena?

A: We hire people with a great mind, and a great eye. Most jobs in VFX require someone to be adept at solving highly technical challenges, while also having an artistic eye. Both sides of the brain are required for this gig.

Q: Your favorite type of project?

A: Oddly enough, although I really enjoy the large popcorn films where we create massive FX and creatures, I have an affinity for some of the smaller projects we are awarded where 'if' the audience doesn't suspect that the film has any computer generated imagery, then we've done our job well. There are lots of films, which don't scream FX, yet use a significant amount of CG to sculpt a feel and aid in the storytelling.

Q: Tell us about the working environment at Luma. Would I be part of a team, working on tasks by myself, fully collaborative? Do you have sleeping pods like Google?

A: Luma is a very different kind of company. We're artist owned and operated. This is an important distinction, in that we wholly understand the craft and what artists and developers need to execute at their highest ability. We're a very human company, we're very careful to support a strong and vibrant culture. Being a staff based model in what is generally a very nomadic field, yields a very strong team, and stability. Many of the people that are with our company have been with us for many years, some since the inception of the studio over a decade ago.

In addition we have an operations staff, and their primary task is to find fun ways to break up the day and make life better for our artists. Luma does huge things for the staff when we wrap a substantial project. For example, Luma took the staff on an all-expenses paid vacation to party in Hawaii for a week. I don't want that to sound extravagant, it's quite the opposite. Much of the money Luma makes goes right back into preserving and expanding our infrastructure, and most importantly our commitment to our staff.

More importantly though, Luma is about all the little things throughout the day, the music, the game room, the atrium sporting a hammock, the sun lit building, no cubicles, no micro management, and above all no stifling of creativity.

Our management is very different as well. We believe in a flat hierarchy, not a dictatorship. In my experience, a lot of companies say they are collaborative, and then you get there and realize how deep the politics run. Luma is different this way. We have a happy staff, and very little to no politics. We put our energy on the screen.

122

I sit out in the artist area at a normal desk just like everyone else. I had an office but gave it up because I didn't like it. I believe management should always be on the floor with whoever is producing the work. Detached management makes poor decisions.

Q: How are VFX specialists compensated? Is it salary, per project, etc.?

A: I have ownership in the company and also receive a salary. I can't answer that for the entire industry but I can say that for our staff of artists and development team, we are well paid, and very well treated.

Q: What is the most challenging part of your projects?

A: Funny enough, they are all very challenging in different ways. I'd say that shows which have digital humans, or animals are amongst the most difficult because everyone subconsciously knows exactly what animals and humans look like, how they move, etc. so the audience has a point of reference and can spot very subtle inaccuracies. Whereas, with a creature or a robot, there is a suspension of disbelief and the audience will let their imaginations take them away.

Q: I understand that most days are different, but would you tell me about a typical day at work for Vince Cirelli?

A: I split my time equally between Los Angeles and Melbourne so, I'm video conferencing either very early in the morning with LA when I'm in Melbourne, or into the late night with Melbourne when I'm in LA.

From there it's syncing with clients, and talking through sequences using various tools which allow us to view footage and make notations to share with multiple parties around the world.

Then I might discuss goals, and scheduling for a show making sure we're all clear on what tasks we have to accomplish for the day. In addition I'll also review and plot through the technical hurdles at the-per shot level with individual technical directors and artists.

There are a lot of moving parts in VFX production, hundreds of elements could go into a single shot, and they all come from different areas of the pipeline. I need to ensure that they are coherent in art direction so that when they are combined they tell the story the filmmakers want to convey.

To compound this, we run multiple movies at once. So in the same day we may be talking about a period 19th century architecture, the kinematics of a horse, and the computationally heavy dynamic simulations required to have a giant creature crash through a wall! My days are always different, always challenging, and very rewarding.

Q: If I were interested in feature film fx what might be the best advice you could give me?

A: Keep your reel and showcase as curated as possible. Meaning, don't put filler work in your portfolio, only include the very best imagery because volume means nothing; quality means everything.

Replicate nature, as much as you can. The human form, and anatomy is the foundation for a lot of the work we do. Most things start there, even the creature work. If it's grounded by the human form, or nature in some way audiences have an easier time believing it, because they connect with it on a subconscious level. Make sure that you don't get lost in the technical side; remember were here to make beautiful imagery.

Q: What was the best time you've ever had working on a film?

A: In the past I have thoroughly enjoyed working on the Coen brother's films. They are amongst my favorite directors. They are very grounded directors who have a distinct and clear vision of their film. Their visual direction is direct and always about facilitating the story telling and nothing else.

Q: What type of education did you have, and did it prepare you for what you do today?

A: I grew up in my grandfather's music store watching him play and repair instruments; he was a real craftsman. My father is a talented musician, and has an engineer's mind. My mother has an artist's eye, and is an avid crafter/maker. Between them all, I was always exposed to multiple forms of art and technology. Because of their combined influences and abilities, I was well equipped for what I ultimately do now.

My wife however, was truly the catalyst. She expected some stability, which wasn't unreasonable, so I gave up an unstable music career and looked to other forms of creativity, which didn't require me, being on the road a lot. I washed dishes by day, and learned about filmmaking, and 3D at night. I taught myself, there were no VFX schools back then.

Q: Does LUMA have interns?

A: Part of our philosophy, is that we look for diamonds in the rough. We give people just starting their careers a chance, if they illustrate that they have a sharp mind, and a good eye then we try to retain that talent and grow it.

Q: What haven't you done that's still on your list - either personally or professionally?

A: There are so many things I want to do, and learn. Some may sound far fetched, some maybe more within reach. If I mention them, you'll think I'm crazy. But, I think imagination and drive is what makes the intangible, tangible.

Q: What should the world know about Vince Cirelli?

A: I'm an geek at heart, love 40s-60s jazz, film, science, technology, fabrication, design, tea boats, the beach, my wonderful wife Aliona and daughter Alyssa.

PROSTHETIC ARTIST

A staggering number of artists work on larger feature film projects, including graphic, digital landscape, character designers, painters…I think one of the more interesting types of artists is the Prosthetic Artist.

VICTORIA BANCROFT

Prosthetic Artist

IMDB – Game of Thrones, Guardian of the Galaxy, Harry Potter, Downtown Abby, Star Wars, Bond, King Arthur

Q: Victoria, I'm a big fan of your work, would you tell me about the life of a Prosthetic Artist?

A: I am a prosthetic make up artist and I work on a huge cross section of both television and film projects. Some are clearly better known than others like *Harry Potter* for example where I was involved in the goblins of Gringotts Bank, and my goodness, there were a lot of them! I think it was the largest prosthetic team to work on a film to date.

Q: There are many different roles a person with the title of 'Special Makeup Artist' might take on. If possible, would you elaborate eon all the possible jobs?

A: Well first of all it's a gargantuan process and my particular roll is last in order!

Those who are in the workshop during pre-filming have roles such as life-casting actors or sculpting, which is what you want the final thing to look like, be it old age, creatures, or blood and guts.

There is also mold making, running pieces (the process of injecting a mould with silicone or gelatin or foam latex so we can see what it is that's being created), painting, hair punching and much, more.

On the set during filming is the point where I step in to fit the prosthetic pieces to the actors This process involves lots of time, patience and glue to ensure each piece is in the correct place and that the edges blend seamlessly into one another, painting the overall prosthetic (including the artist underneath it all). The goal of this process is to include as much detail as possible to make close up shooting possible. I then remain on set with the actors during the shoot to ensure nothing goes wrong.

Q: Was there a special person, or event that encouraged you to pursue a career in the film industry?

A: As a teenager I was learning dance and when working towards a particular dance show we were sent to 'Charles Fox' in Covent Garden, London for a day of training about how to do our make up. I loved it so much that I started investigating make-up as a career. I studied Theatre Arts and as I progressed moved on to the London College of Fashion to do a specific course ... that was over 20 years ago.

Q: Tell me about working with Actors and Actresses?

A: My role is very specific to them so it's really important (in my opinion) to try and be perceptive to their needs and personalities. We are literally in their faces, invading their personal space, for hours on end from very early morning and at times when they are trying to do their own jobs. I have had the pleasure of working with some big names and I love my role in aiding them all to become the character in a more complete way.

Q: Do you make a good living in your profession?

A: The hours are long, the conditions are not always the most desirable and the days start early so whatever your role within this industry, you must first and foremost love your job because it is all consuming. Rates of pay are hugely variable depending on the genre and the budget of the show/ movie. It's certainly possible to make a very good living but being freelance isn't an easy option. Make good connections and make yourself indispensable!

Q: Tell us something that most people wouldn't know about a Prosthetic Makeup Artist on a big budget production?

A: One minute we could be dealing with the delicate old age prosthetic and the fine details around the eyes and mouth with careful fine painting the next we could be lugging intestines and gallons of blood around a set! Variety is the spice of life!

Q: Do you *pay it forward* and help newbies in the business?

A: There are often trainees / interns around and I relish that because it's so important to learn through experience in the film business. Formal training can not prepare you for the on set hierarchy among departments nor can it teach you about working under big-time pressure and in professional conditions.

Q: What is the most challenging part of your job?

A: I would have to say the hours and general conditions! Our job is done first, so if an actor is going into hair, makeup and costume they all happen after the prosthetics are in place. We are always working to a deadline for set by the 1st assistant director for when an actor must be present on set. Once the artist is on set our job is to be there, watching, touching up and tweaking to maintain the prosthetic and actor at the highest level throughout the 12-hour shooting schedule.

The conditions of the set can also be somewhat of a challenge. We are sometimes outside in the middle of the night when it's windy, raining and cold making it uncomfortable and harder to do our job. Alternatively, we get to be on set during the beautiful sunny days in amazing places, like Scotland!

Q: Some words of wisdom?

A: Stick with it, soak up all the information you can, smile a lot and just do whatever you can to be helpful. After 20 years I still love it, every single day!

LOCATION MANAGER

My wife's family has long been a partner in the Charles 'R' Ranch south of Santa Fe, New Mexico where we have enjoyed spending time for many years. It's a working ranch that raises Corrientes cattle, the breed that are often associated with rodeos for such events as roping. The ranch has also been a film location for many major Hollywood releases.

A few of years ago, while driving to the ranch, I saw a large encampment about two miles out on top of one of the hills. There were several semis, tents, heavy equipment and hundreds of people roaming the wooded area.

We came to find that the Coen Brothers were shooting *True Grit*, and when we visited the set, I had the opportunity to speak with Tyson Bidner, the Chief location manager. He told me that he had found this location on a website and when he presented it to the Coen brothers for the mineshaft scene, they thought it was perfect.

There was only one problem. The canyon cliff where they wanted to shoot had no access road ... What do you do when you can't get equipment and actors to the set, but you have a $38,000,000 budget? You bring in heavy excavating equipment and build a road ... fast!

I've never seen anything like it, a two lane gravel road was constructed in just a couple of days, the film's scenes shot, and then the road was de-constructed, trees planted, and you wouldn't know the crew of 200 set foot on the ranch. If I hadn't seen it for myself, I would never have believed it. So goes the job of a location manager.

MARK KAMINE
Location manager

IMDB - Sopranos, 42, American Hustle, Silver Linings Playbook, Shutter Island

Q: Mark, I ran into a location scout on the set of "True Grit", which was being shot in Las Vegas, NM and he told me that he has one of the most interesting jobs in the film business, do you agree?

A: It's great because you have creative input early on – sometimes you're the first person at a location that will be used in the movie, and while you're not deciding (that'll be the production designer and director), you can have creative impact.

Then you get to be involved in the art department prep of locations, the rigging of lights before the company shoots there, the shooting, and the wrapping out of the location – so it gives you a broad picture of what goes on.

Q: Do you negotiate the contracts with property owners?

A: Yes, you negotiate the deals, with property owners and also with local and other government entities. You'll talk to town councils, police, fire department, anyone you need to get permission from to film.

As for property owners, there's usually a ballpark fee for a certain geographical area. A New York City or Los Angeles homeowner - or storeowner is going to get more money than someone in a small town in the middle of the country. You budget based on prior knowledge, local expertise, etc.

Normally you would tell people how many days you'll be there for prepping, shooting and wrapping, and figure out a fee per day, with shoot days worth more (more of an invasion of privacy on those days). You might also pay for dog sitting, or if it's a real takeover of a place, you'll put them up in a hotel, and give a per diem so they can eat and all that while they're not home. Then you sign a contract, get an insurance certificate, and start the process.

Q: Are you the liaison between the film's management and local film commissions?

A: As a location manager you are dealing with film commissions all the time. They can be very helpful and are usually great resources – they'll know who to talk to in local governments and who to call if you need help.

Q: How did you get your start in the business?

A: To get my first job on a mainstream movie, I worked for free for producer Michael Nozik, essentially doing data entry, answering phones and running errands. One of his projects was getting off the ground, and he said he'd try to get me on it if it happened. It was *Quiz Show* and within weeks I was driving a 15-passenger van with Robert Redford sitting in the passenger seat. I remember we were driving along and Redford was talking about how you could live in New York City your whole life and then one day find yourself lost in some part of Manhattan you've never seen before. Then he looked directly at me and said, "Like you might be now." And, in fact, I had been trying to get the location manager's attention for a while. Because I *was* lost!

Q: What were the best and worst deals you've made on a location?

A: I think my best deals are deals where the home or business owner goes through the prep and shoot and wrap and feels fairly compensated. It can be kind of a shock when 150 people show up on filming day. You want to warn them, and not just play up the glamour of filmmaking.

On *Sopranos* I had to make yearly deals for the pork store location once we got going. It wasn't cheap but once the deal was done, the owner was happy and we had free access for the five or six months of filming; a pretty valuable asset.

On the same show, I also made some bad deals because there were locations where we had to return over and over and the owners had us over a barrel and knew it. It was a losing battle.

Q: Tell me something that most people don't know about the job of a Location Manager.

A: The details of the job are probably something you wouldn't think about. It's one thing to find the locations where the designer and director want to shoot but once that's done the real work begins. How many days does the art department need there before shooting starts, where do all the trucks park so the actors and equipment are close but not in the shot? What kind of permit do you need from the municipality? How much do police cost?

Q: What was the strangest location anyone ever asked you to find, and were you able to deliver?

A: During *Sopranos* we were asked to find possible "body dump sites" and then left to our own imagination, so we had this big file ready to go.

Q: Are you still active as a Location Manager, or was it a stepping-stone to other parts of the industry?

A: Definitely a stepping-stone. It's a good one, because you can have a pretty big staff for a film department as well as a decent budget, so you have to learn to effectively manage people and money. You also spend time with the designers and directors, so you get to work with creative, which is a big part of production managing and producing.

Q: What is the most challenging part of the Location Manager's job?

A: Different jobs present different challenges but one thing that stays the same is that as a location manager you are at the forefront of dealing with the impact of the movie on the public.

So when you're taking over a house or business, taking parking on a street, asking people not to walk where they're used to walking, and all the rest of the intrusions of filming on location, you end up caught between the production (which wants full freedom to do whatever it wants when it wants), and the public, including governmental authorities, police, residents, business owners and customers, all of whom might be curious about movie stars but have a different set of priorities. You have to be persuasive, and you also have to be the one to deliver the bad news to production sometimes, for example that you can't just shut down a New York City avenue on a weekday for 12 hours!

Q: Mark, do you ever get the chance to help people get into the business?

A: I'm often helping people get into the business, somewhat reluctantly, because it's not the easiest career, but if you want to work on productions who am I to stop you? It's always a pleasure when someone gets it … works hard, listens, learns.

In an industry where a select few make millions of dollars, there are the thousands of crew members that climb out of bed in the wee hours of the morning before the sun decides to show itself and make their way to the set. Many of these people have multiple jobs and work in a variety of positions so they can stay busy and in the game. Samuel Adler has held the job of Location Scout, Accounting clerk, Assistant director, producer, as well as been part of the camera department.

SAMUEL ADLER

Location Scout

IMDB - Hall Pass, Orange is the New Black, The Watch, Due Date, Beyond the Pale

Q: Sam, how do you get hired as a Location Scout?

A: Like most things in the production world it's mostly word of mouth and whom you know. The more you work the more your name will get around and the more you will work! Usually a fellow location colleague will call me, and on a good day a producer will call.

Q: Location scouting seems like a cool job, what exactly are you responsible for?

A: We find available places and take photos that fit several creative and logistical elements

134

that the film requires. We then present these options to the key creative people who will make the decisions based on a number of deceive factors that fall somewhere between the best creative fit and the films budget and operational needs.

A simple way of explaining it is that the job is finding a location that the director and production designer see in their heads. Sometimes they don't even know what that is until you show them. Needless to say it's a creative process.

Q: Do most location scouts get hired to work in specific geographic locations – like their hometown?

A: Yes, I would say the core of location people are based geographically. Time is money in the film industry and hiring someone who lives in the area and knows it well saves time and brings about the best results.

Q: At what point are you brought in to the process and whom do you work most closely with?

A: When working as a location scout I can be brought in as soon as the producer has the script and has money in the bank, or later down the road in preproduction when most of the locations have been found and its time to start the prep work. At that point I become an assistant location manager and work with other assistant department heads and coordinators

The locations department has several moving parts within each department of the film and it's crucial that a clear line of communication is established early on. Best Boys want to know if it's okay to run cable or hang lights somewhere with the owner's permission. Set dressers want to know when they can get access to the set to get it ready for shooting. Construction must restore a location to the way they found it. And transportation wants to know where they can park all the trucks and trailers.

Q: How are location scouts compensated?

A: For tv and film it's based on a daily rate.

Q: Are there multiple location managers or scouts that work on a single project?

A: One manager will always supervise several scouts. Everyone on the location team has the ability to scout but some are hired only as scouts. Every now and then the location PA will scout. This is how you learn the business.

Department Structure (Every show is different based on budget and other variables)

Location Manager
- Key Assistant location manager (Key ALM)
- Assistant location manager (ALM – There can be more then one)
- Location Scout (Brought in to scout and then leaves show. No set work)
- Location Coordinator (handles departments paperwork and permits)
- Location Assistant (Same as a Location PA but is union)
- Location PA

Q: Do you have an agent, or do you market yourself?

A: No agent. Only the above the line people (producers, writers, directors), occasional key department heads (costumes and art), and talent have agents.

It's all based on word of mouth and trust circles as it has been done for decades. There are what they call 'source books' that are published in each state and you can pay to get your name in them. But I've never personally done it.

Q: Sam, do you have some general advice, thoughts, or tips for my readers?

A: I believe I might Michael, here goes…
Film work is 90% operations and only 10% art! Most of the crew is not hired for their creative and artistic vision. They are hired to carry out the vision and direction of someone else. 10% of the crew (department heads) control 90% of the creative direction.

So if you're some hotshot director or DP just out of film school, I have a rude wake up call for you. You are going to start out as a PA and no one will care how creative you are. We do care how good you are at solving problems and working hard at any task given to you. Stay humble and work hard and you will get there.

Sam continues …

Take care of your boss, and your boss will take care of you!

There's no HR department in the freelance world. Hiring and firing comes from the department head or the assistant department head. You are there to make their jobs easier but I'm not talking about brown nosing. What I am talking about is making sure you always look after your department and remembering that your actions reflect those of your boss. You're a member of a team, and you need to take pride in that. You succeed together and you fail together. No joke…

Small real life example…

When I was getting started I always made sure I carried a few spare cellphone chargers with me for different types of phones. Why? At some point my boss will forget to bring theirs and I will be right there ready to help. It has happened several times on different shows. Keeping my boss operational is always a good way to look out for the team.

Department heads like to build great teams that work well with each other. When they find people they like, they try to keep them together and go from project to project. That's one way to stay employed.

My department head walks into the office and announces, "In my opinion this is the dream team on the dream job. I want everyone back for next season"

With that in mind, people travel in circles when it comes to working together. Lots of famous directors and producers work with the same people on every film they make. Why break in a new team when you have a winning formula? So getting in with the right people on the right team is particularly crucial for your long-term career goals.

So if you want to work on films but you keep getting tv gigs? Check your circles; career advice for later on down the line. If you want to write or develop for tv and film move to LA. LA is losing production jobs but its still the king of content creation.

Hiring tip:

Jobs offers come at the oddest times. When I was a set PA I would get calls at midnight to be on set in 6 hrs. You need to be ready to pick up the phone and be ready to work when they need you. Most of the time there's no job interview. Someone put your name out there and that was good enough. Good luck!

GAFFER

Like most of us, from time to time I worry about my lighting bill, but can you imagine getting one for a single night of shooting when the director calls for it to look like mid-day with full sun! That easily costs as much as a month's electric bill for a small neighborhood. The responsibility of fulfilling a directors vision on shoot day is riding on many shoulders, but none more than on the gaffer, sometimes called the chief lighting technician.

When I was soliciting crew to share their thoughts I received many great responses and a few standouts. Jerry Enright is one of them. He is a long time veteran of the film industry and eager to help the next generation.

JERRY ENRIGHT

Gaffer

IMDB - Sex and the City, Robin Hood, The Peacemaker, Dream Corp LLC

Q: Jerry, you're a funny guy with a wealth of experience. Would you tell me exactly what a Gaffer does in some detail?

A: The gaffer on a movie set is in charge of lighting the actors and sets. As a gaffer, I am hired for the production phase only and my responsibilities would begin with reading the script and breaking it down by location, manpower and equipment.

The planning phase of the picture usually determines the difference between success and failure. I'm a stickler for detail and try to plan for every outcome, which is impossible because I've never worked on a film that went exactly as planned.

For example, I worked, as a rigging gaffer on *Fire in The Sky* in Roseburg, Oregon and the location for the alien abduction scene was a remote, steep, mountain meadow with limited fire road access. While scouting with the production team, the director looking through his viewfinder said he wanted to shoot in three directions. The fourth direction was where I was to put my equipment. This was very important information to me because the "equipment" was a 100 ft. crane with the lights used to simulate the spacecraft. The crane was gigantic and yellow, and I was to rig a 60 ft. x 40 ft. rock and roll truss with 20/10k maxi brutes (each light uses ten thousand watts). This was a massive, complicated rig. The cable to power all these lights was an engineering nightmare and we had to buy 500 ft. of extra cable so the crane could lift the added weight. It took my local crew over two weeks to get ready for the abduction scene and it was a brutal schedule.

I had very little contact with the shooting crew at this time as we literally dug the crane into the side of the mountain with an earthmover. On a fire road above the crane I placed the twin 1500 amp generators so they would be as far away as possible for the sound recording; so this required over 700 ft. of heavy cable.

The first night of shooting the abduction rolls around, and after two straight weeks of rigging the set, I was pretty good and then... The director strolls onto the set, looks toward the crane and says," I want to shoot in that direction, can we move that big yellow thing?" I can't remember exactly what I said, but I'm positive it started with the letter "F".
I then explained that we could NOT, under any circumstances, move "the big yellow thing." And suggested that we instead mask the crane with camouflaged nets and have the greens department cover it with foliage. Once he calmed down, our director admitted this was a workable solution. Problem solved.

The moral is, the gaffer is always light on his feet and can change direction easily. Stay calm and don't get rattled. Expect things to change.

Q: What's the difference between the title of *Gaffer* and a *Chief Lighting Technician*?

A: There is no difference between the term gaffer and chief lighting technician. They are one in the same. The reason gaffer was changed to chief lighting technician was my union, IATSE, Hollywood Set Lighting, Local 728, thought chief lighting technician sounded more professional.

Q: At what point do you go to work?

A: As gaffer, I am hired directly by the director of photography or DP. Once the DP has a job, he or she, would call me and say we have the film. I would then meet with the line producer or UPM and work out a deal. The deal would include rate of pay, box rental, equipment rental and some discussion of manpower needs. This portion is always a dance, because the UPM always cries poor (it's part of their job). I've learned to be agreeable to a point but gently get my way. This method is especially helpful when asking for manpower or specialized (expensive) equipment.

The conversation sometimes goes like this…
    I say, " the DP needs a certain light and I need the manpower to make it happen."
    The UPM says, "We just don't have it in the budget."
    I say, "OK, I'll tell my Academy Award winning DP that you say we don't have a
    budget for his vision."

When unburdened by money worries, I am truly free to paint with light.

Q: How important are relationships and attitude on set?

A: Relationships on any film are Paramount (capitalized because Paramount Pictures is my break in lot).

My advice is to always show up early, be prepared and NEVER mistreat the PA's (lowly production assistants who routinely move into producer/director roles). I can't tell you how many times this has happened, but I've seen it more than once! In fact, a surly attitude has no place on the film set. Point is, since a picture is such a collaborative art, no one is expendable. Everyone contributes; even the extras (also known as "props that eat").

Speaking of extras here's a short story. I was a young, cocky, full of myself set lighting electrician on a big picture. I looked down on all PAs and extras and was not subtle with my disdain. One day at lunch after going through the catering line with food tray in hand, I snatched a chair from an older extra just as she was getting ready to sit down. She had set her tray down and was going to join her friends. We had a lot of extras this day and chairs were at a premium. Needless to say, she wasn't real happy with me, but I couldn't have cared less. I took my food tray and "my" chair and joined my union brothers for lunch on the electric truck. We were laughing about the incident until the 1st AD (assistant director), motioned to me to talk. He told me that the woman whose chair I had stolen happened to be the producer's wife. She was not a professional extra and just thought it would be fun to be in his movie. He also informed me that if I didn't return the chair with a heartfelt apology, I would be immediately terminated!

From that day on, I realized that playing well with others was my most important job description. It takes a village to make movie magic.

Q: Do you work long days as a Gaffer?

A: Long hours are always a part of movie making. Because of contractual restraints, most actors are booked for a block of time that fits their busy schedule and when problems arise the shooting schedule can get pushed by a few days or even weeks. When this happens, the crew usually suffers long, brutal hours to make up time lost.

Sometimes, if the director has a lot of clout and can do no wrong we will work long hours just to support their creativity. Ridley Scott on the first day of a well-known movie shot for over sixteen hours to establish his pace and weed out any weakness in the crew. I respected him greatly for his leadership and creative skills. He is a master.

Expect long hours. Sleep whenever and wherever possible.

Q: Could you tell me about a typical day on the set?

A: After arriving on location and parking I jump in a shuttle van and head to my electric truck, which is usually close to the set. Typically, the rigging crew would start 4-5 hours before the shooting crew and have all the lights and cable ready to go. Any last minute changes would be implemented and if satisfied, I would join the crew for a catered breakfast.

Around ten minutes before call time I ask my 'Best Boy' (my closest assistant in charge of men and equipment) to fire the generator and power up the set.

I would have already discussed with my DP what we would be shooting, who we are shooting, which direction and how he wanted to light it. The first day on the set is usually awkward for a couple of turnarounds but once the grips and electricians (Set Lighting Technicians) are working as a team, things go very smoothly. After around 10-12 hours of shooting, the 1st AD calls for the martini shot (last shot of the day) and the 2nd AD will hand out the next days call sheet and shooting schedule. The set is made safe for the night, and if we are starting in the same set up the next day, a general announcement is made that we have a "hot set". Nothing is to be moved and we walk away. I go to the electric truck, take off my meter belt, thank the boys for the days hustle and go home. Repeat 40 or 50 times! That's my day.

Q: What type of education did you have?

A: My education is ongoing. Yes, it's true I have a college degree but in my end of the film business, my degree is more of a hindrance than a positive. The reason is simple. Most of the people I work with do not have a degree and I found it was easier to conform by not talking about it. But make no mistake; my college education changed my life. I feel my education has given me a distinct advantage. Having a degree proves that you can finish. It proves you can, not only learn things, but that you know HOW to learn. And this directly relates to everyday life. When we stop learning, we are deceased.

Q: Is the job of a Gaffer a viable long-term career?

A: Yes, a career as gaffer is a viable, long-term career no question. But I was fortunate to enter the biz when Hollywood was flying high. Hollywood is a confusing place now. Films are no longer filmed. High definition video cameras are commonplace. Computer generated images or CGI, is advancing so fast, I see a future without organic actors. I rode the wave at the perfect time.

Computers have taken over. Filmmaking is changing at a breakneck pace but what will never change is the need for skilled, professional film crew. Advanced cameras and techniques always need human touch.

I also spoke with Gaffer, Michael Ambrose, who was busy on the production of '*Mad Men*' but had a little time to share some of what he has learned working with many world-renowned cinematographers on the largest productions in Hollywood. He says there is nowhere in the non-union world to learn how the big studio movies are lit, so being on a rigging crew was the key to his advancement in the industry.

MICHAEL AMBROSE

Gaffer

IMDB - Captain America, Mad Men, Homeland, Furious 7, The Expendables, Lucifer, Jason Bourne, Fast 8, Kong Skull Island, Black Panther

Q: Michael, what is a Gaffer?

A: Many times when asked what I do for a living I receive strange looks when I say, "I am a gaffer". They sometimes have an idea of what a gaffer does, "Oh yeah, you work in the movies, I've seen that in the credits!" Then they ask, "What exactly does a gaffer do?"

Being the gaffer is a great job as it mixes management, technical, and creative in a unique way. The gaffer is the head of the set lighting department on a movie, television show, commercial, music video, etc. I work very closely with the cinematographer, or DP. Front row seat on the movie set! I collaborate with them to determine lighting styles, color, angle, shadows, equipment, and placement.

In addition I work with the head of the grip department known as the Key Grip. Together we do our best to bring the directors, writers, and producers vision to reality. Needless to say there is rarely a dull moment as every project, scene, and shot is different, as well as the people we work with. I'm also responsible for all electrical power and distribution on the set, practical lighting which we coordinate and collaborate with the set decoration department, generators for electrical power, and coordinating with the teamsters in the transportation department to make sure all equipment is where it needs to be when it needs to be.

I answer to the unit production manager regarding labor and equipment budgets, and attend production meetings before shooting begins to represent the set lighting department on all pre production planning and location scouting. I travel a lot as many movies are shot in various locations around the world.

Q: Would you tell me about your team?

A: I have a staff that varies in size depending on the size of the project. The Best Boy Electric is my assistant who organizes crew, equipment, and paperwork amongst many other responsibilities while I'm busy on set.

On most productions I also coordinate a rigging crew, which works ahead and behind the shooting crew pre-rigging and lighting to help us stay on schedule and work efficiently. My rigging gaffer, who also has a rigging best boy electric, heads the rigging crew up. I will usually have 3-5 set lighting technicians on set with me. More are sometimes added as needed for specialty lighting like lights up in aerial lifts or rooftops.

The rigging crew will also have anywhere from 3-15 set lighting technicians additionally. On some shows we also have a 'Fixtures Department' which will handle all wiring and electrical for on camera lighting. This is done in collaboration with the art department and set decorators as well as the prop department.

Q: How did you get your start?

A: Growing up in Southern California, I was interested in lighting for theatre in High School. That led to an early career in entertainment lighting for theatre, music, and corporate events. In 1990 I moved into the Hollywood area and befriended a neighbor who happened to be a cinematographer.

That relationship connected me with jobs in the non-union independent scene; eventually I joined IATSE Local 728, and from there I just showed up, smiled, did my best to be personable and helpful.

Q: Would you talk about your relationship with the DP?

A: One of the best parts of being a gaffer is the working closely with the DP to achieve the look of a film. This collaboration is unique to the art of filmmaking, which I believe to be one of the most collaborative forms of expression in art.

For example in the latest *Star Trek* movies directed by JJ Abrams, cinematographer Dan Mindel A.S.C., wanted anamorphic flares to hit the lens periodically through the film. This became one of the iconic "looks" of the new franchise.

While we were shooting scenes it was important to get these flares in just the right place, and time them with camera movement and actor blocking. In order to achieve the effect I would stand right on the bitter edge of frame with a high powered Xenon flashlight and hit the lens at the exact moment, then usually have to duck out of the way just in time before I would be caught in the shot. This was very satisfying because I knew I was totally immersed in the process with all the other filmmakers including the actors, director, DP, etc

By the way, while talking about *Star Trek*, I must admit the first time I stepped onto the bridge of the Starship Enterprise; it had to be one of the most exciting moments of my career. The set was spectacular, and you could actually imagine taking off across the galaxy and yes, I did sit in the captain's chair!

Q: Tell me about your workday?

A: Long days are part of the job. Our workweek generally ranges between 60-90 hours depending on the project. The disadvantage of long shooting days is that I may come to work at 7 am on Monday, but other crews, actors, stunts, and the cinematographer, have 12 hour turn-a-rounds to rest, my call might get pushed everyday. So by Friday I could be coming to work at 11 am or later! Consequently Fridays work moves into Saturday, which we unaffectionately call "Fraturday". We don't like Fraturdays!

Q: Are there residuals for a Gaffer?

A: There are no residuals for gaffers. The residuals we would have received are now contributed to our pension fund from what I understand. So, I suppose in a way we still may benefit from them. There is a set pay scale in the union contract and it fluctuates depending on project and budget. Often times an 'above scale' rate will be negotiated for large studio feature films and commercials.

Q: What's the hardest part of your job?

A: I think one of the most challenging things we have to do in cinematography is shoot in "no light" circumstances. I've have had directors that inform they want it black, dark, no light sources anywhere! Well, we still need to expose the image somehow. There is 'dark', and then there is fired!

During filming of some of the dramatically darker moments in the television series *Mad Men*, Christopher Manley A.S.C. and I came up against this challenge several times. Creator Mathew Weiner made it clear he wanted the characters in the scene to be completely in the dark. Sometimes we could motivate a light from a hallway or a bathroom with a cracked door. Sometimes, there were no light sources available.

I have often said that when lighting a completely dark scene we use more lighting instruments then a scene with motivated light sources. We solve these problems in various ways; sometimes we use an overhead soft source with many stops under exposed, so there is just enough to see some highlight and shadows that separate the black spaces in the frame.

146

Sometimes we just put a "moonlight" edge on everything, but we have to be careful it doesn't look too "Hollywood". Even though it's fake, we don't want to draw attention to it. Other times our best work is when you don't notice what we did anything. You should be drawn into the story that's being told.

Q: If I were an aspiring Lighting Tech what's your best advice?

A: I am often asked this question and I always give the same advice. If you want to direct, direct, if you want to be a cinematographer, then shoot, if you want to be a gaffer, then start directing the lighting on any project you can get your hands on.

Say 'Yes' to everything in the beginning. Build your network, and just practice your craft. There are however limits to moving up, and promotions are rarely successful. There are so many levels of production coupled with budget tiers. Start on lower budget projects and work your way up the project/budget ladder.

Q: When you're working on a very popular show like *Mad Men*, is it almost like a day job?

A: Episodic television is a production factory. I like feature films, where you work on a story line for 3-6 months then move on to a new story. That said, *Mad Men* was quite unique. The writing was exceptional and it was a perfect storm for creating iconic imagery as well as a wonderful ensemble in front of and behind the camera. Of course, revisiting the same set over and over again can get old, but *Mad Men* was only 13 episodes a season, and it was closer to a feature schedule in terms of commitment, about 5-6 months.

I worked feature projects between seasons until the last 'Mad Men' season when my feature overlapped the start date, so I had to pass. I am grateful and fortunate to have been the gaffer for 6 full seasons on 'Mad Men'.

Q: Have you ever had an intern?

A: I have helped out on some student films and thought the DP might one day be successful We have stayed in touch and he recently hired me for a national commercial he was shooting! I've attempted to bring interns on the set, and it is almost always shot down by production. I think that is a shame. I would like to do more mentoring.

Q: Do you have a favorite film?

A: My most memorable moment on a film has to be while working with Phedon Papamichael A.S.C. on the film *The Pursuit of Happyness*. We were in an office building in San Francisco filming the end of the movie where the main character portrayed by Will Smith, 'Chris Gardner', is called into the office to be told he had won the job after quite the life struggle and against all odds. It was an incredibly emotional scene and Will Smith was spectacular. I was in my usual position, right behind the camera, front row seat, watching the scene unfold live in front of me. It was amazing to see Will perform his craft. There wasn't a dry eye in the room when that scene was finished.

KEY GRIP

In the past I have often mixed up the titles of Key Grip and Gaffer because they sounded so similar. Finally, Michael Catanzarite comes along and clears it up for me. Key Grip is a cool job, but if you decide to take it on, you'd better be ready for some hard work, both mentally and physically.

MICHAEL CATANZARITE

Key Grip

IMDB – Titanic, Mad Men, The Mentalist, Bruce Almighty, The Forgotten, Lucifer

Q: Michael, talk to us about the job of the Key Grip?

A: The key grip is the head of the grip department and has a second that is called the best boy (female or male). The number of grips under the key grip can range from one to well over fifty. The size is of the grip crew is based upon the size of the job, the timeframe for completion, and the project budget.

The duties of this department are to support the camera and lighting departments.

Our camera duties include the placing for static or moving shots to capture the action of the scene where the camera may be on a tripod or a dolly; a steady cam or a crane. If the camera were to be set in the gutter of the street, we would have a grip there to level the camera and provide comfort for the camera assistant and operator. One of my personal favorites was strapping camera to a horse saddle for a galloping shot!

We also provide lighting support, which includes the control, softening, coloring, and placement of the lamps used to light the scenes. Material and gelatin frames are used to create different moods and emotions with the light by changing the quality of the illumination. Black colored material is used to control the light from going in directions that are unintended. Sand bags are used to make the lights safe as well as ladders to reach higher positions. In some cases a platform may need to be fabricated to bring the light several stories in the air. My favorite lighting rig is to put the light in a 100 ft. construction crane and use it as a "moon" source for night scenes.

Q: People unfamiliar with your job often mix it up with a gaffer. Would you explain the difference?

A: The gaffer, or chief lighting technician, is the head of the lighting department. He is the equal of the key grip. The lighting technician, the key grip and the director of photography form the holy trinity of lighting.

Q: Do you start work on a project at the beginning of production?

A: Any key grip will tell you that he is always brought on a project too late and while it's a universal complaint, it does have some merit. The design of the every set should be done with the ability to light the set top of mind, however this is usually not the case. Time is money in the film business and the input of every department head can be valuable, particularly if it affects the scope and efficiency of the project. If for example, a set is built on a riser to mimic an apartment, it will impact the amount and type of equipment needed which shouldn't come as a surprise, but somehow always does.

We are generally brought in, at the very least, to do a technical scout of the locations and/or stages. This lets us know what to expect and what to order. Any pre-rigs will be set up at this time. Next we load the gear from a rental house into a semi-truck that will become our office on wheels and mix and match the gear to overcome any lighting or camera obstacle we encounter.

It is often helpful during this week or two of prep to do a camera test with the camera for the actors and their wardrobe. A check of the makeup and hair under real lighting is also beneficial.

Q: Michael, as the Key Grip who do you answer to?

A: The key grip works directly for the director of photography but we serve many masters (producers, directors, actors) who all feel it's *their* job to tell you how to do *your* job. However, it's the cameraman that hires us and counts on us to rig every single light that he selects as well as the camera on every shot of the show. The best relationships happen when the key grip is trusted to be an extra set of eyes for the DP. They are truly brothers in light.

Q: Could you walk me through a typical day on the set?

A: Our day begins at *call*. That's the time the crew is told to be on set. The *Call Sheet* includes other relevant information like how to get to the location and where to park. A breakfast is typically served prior to the call time and then we will go to work or be transported to the actual shooting location. We always try to park our equipment truck as close to the set as possible to provide for complete and rapid support.

The call sheet will also tell you what we are supposed to be shooting but it is often in flux. You must remember that we are working with artists and it would not be advisable to tell Tarantino that we can't shoot what he wants because we were not given the proper notice and are unprepared!

On a normal day we will shoot for six hours and then break for a lunch and with any luck we will only shoot six more hours after lunch to complete the days work. Unfortunately, is often it takes up to fifteen hours to get the work done. During this overtime we are receiving double time pay, which is nice, but it's viewed as *blood money*.

Q: Union vs. non-union?

A: The vast majority of work for the grip is done under union contracts. The non-union world is a 'Wild West' where anything goes so I won't bother trying to apply common sense to something that doesn't make any sense.

The studios have collective bargaining agreements in place that dictate a minimum pay scale for each guild. These amounts can be negotiated higher but never lower. There are several different contracts and pay scales that have come to cover the vast differences in budgets. (On a small show you will make less money)

We are compensated *Straight time* for he first 8 hours, *Time and a Half* until 12 hours, (not including lunch), and *Double time* there after.

Q: Michael, what's the best time you've ever had working on a film?

A: The most rewarding experience I've had filmmaking was also the most challenging. In the fall of 2005 a group of grips went to the state of Veracruz, Mexico to make *Appocalypto* with Mel Gibson. What was scheduled as a four-month movie but took nine and a half months to complete. The movie was entirely funded by Gibson's production company with the profits from his self-released *Passion of the Christ*.

There was no studio to answer to and no producers to hurry him along. Mel was the proverbial ten thousand pound gorilla. The major challenge was making a movie in a foreign country with foreign workers speaking a foreign language. To his credit and downfall, we left no location until Mr. Gibson was completely satisfied with the performances and I believe that the work stands alone as an earnest motion picture with a heart and a good message about society.

One of a multitude of issues was during the river-crossing scene. Our camera was covered in a splash bag to prevent the water from ruining it and we had to get it close to the water but also keep it running. The extreme heat and humidity kept shutting the camera off so its fans could engage and keep it from blowing up. The bottom line was that we couldn't get the shots we needed of the villagers crossing the river so we rigged a tube of nitrogen that could be run down the crane arm and fed into the camera bag. This little rig would periodically shoot some cold gas into the camera bag and cool it down. *Problem solved.*

Q: What type of education did you have?

A: I chose to go to college because I thought it is always a good idea to prepare yourself for anything that life might bring you. A good general education will serve you no matter what you do but it didn't have any bearing on my getting into the film industry. It has however come to be a deterrent as less educated people can be intimidated by more educated ones.

Q: Do you see the job of a Grip as a viable long-term career?

A: I wouldn't necessarily recommend my job to anyone; it is not for the meek. Long hours of physical work and being away from your family are an acquired taste. You won't become famous either. Being thanked is rare, but you will be blamed for the failures of others as well as always wondering where your next job will come from.

Q: Last words?

A: True story!
The director John Ford was asked if he were trapped on a desert island and could pick anyone on earth want to be there with him whom would he choose. He quickly replied, "my key grip," When asked why, he said, "If there was any way off the island, he would find it and if there wasn't, we would have a hell of a time until we died!"

LOCATION AUDIO

I had limited experience as a production audio recordist but I can tell you first hand it can be a tough job, not so much physically but as a problem solver. The challenges start from the moment a production is *green-lit* and you get the call from a producer saying, "Hey Michael, we would like to hire you for our film."

You look at the storyboards and see that there is nowhere to properly place microphones to capture the dialogue or action. To some people, this would be too much pressure, but it was heaven for me. A new problem to solve every 10 minutes … it never gets boring!

Jeff Wexler is an award winning production sound mixer with over 80 films to his credit, including *42, Mission Impossible*, and an Oscar nomination for *The Last Samurai*. Jeff lectures about production sound techniques, invents sound recording rigs, and is very dedicated to his chosen profession.

JEFF WEXLER

Location Audio

IMDB - Fight Club, 42, We Bought a Zoo, Rush Hour, Horrible Bosses, Aloha

Q: Jeff, being a long time audio guy myself I understand how important your job is to the filmmaking process. Would you explain what you do?

A: The majority of my career has been as a production sound mixer. The production sound mixer is the person responsible for the principle and primary audio recording during production. Everything that needs to be recorded, dialog, effects, music, voice over narration, on the day while a project is shooting, that is our responsibility. What we record in production is the foundation for all of the work that will go into creating the soundtrack.

Q: How long do you typically work on a project?

A: It varies, but I mostly work on medium to high budget feature films and am usually on the job for about 3 months. Usually, the production sound mixer is only on the job during the shooting schedule, but there are exceptions when one's involvement in a project extends beyond just the production.

For example, on the film *Being There*, I did the productions sound mixing but was also involved in Postproduction phase and re-recording.

Q: How does the job of the production sound mixer differ from an audio engineer that works in a studio?

A: The main difference is our working environment. An "in studio" audio engineer works inside with equipment in a fixed installation with a large-scale console and infinitely more control over the recording environment. The audio engineer who works "in production" has to be prepared to record sound in a wide variety of environments and working conditions.

More importantly, there is a significant difference in the challenges we face on a daily basis Those working in production (and this applies to all the production crafts not just sound) have to be very creative problem solvers and have a high degree of flexibility; not only with the gear we use but the very way we use it.

Q: Would you run me through an abbreviated version of ramping up for a job?

A: First off, I am offered a job and sent a script to read over and then have an interview. If I land the job and we agree on the rates of pay, I will conduct a script breakdown for sound which goes out to all those involved: the director, the production manager, 1st ad, property master, location manager, music coordinator and so forth.

I also make sure that I am involved in tech scouts of the locations and sets in preproduction, and I usually try to have a meeting with postproduction sound people before we start shooting.

Q: You've worked on about a million films, are there any standouts in your mind?

A: I have lots and lots movies where we had fun and made really good movies, and some where we didn't have much fun but made good movies. Of course, there have also been jobs that have been lots of fun and turned out to be really bad movies as well.

Bound For Glory was very important for me since it was my first Union movie. I had done a bunch of low budget non-union movies and been struggling for years to get into the Union (the I.A.T.S.E.) so I would be able to do better movies. I had just joined the I.A. when I was offered *Bound For Glory* but just days before starting the movie, the I.A. decided to prevent me from doing the movie (I was in the wrong seniority group so not technically allowed to take the job). Director, Hal Ashby came to my aid and locked himself in his hotel room on location in Stockton, California, and told the producers he wasn't coming out until he was assured that I was on the job… problem solved!

It was the biggest challenge of my relatively new career and had a 6 month shooting schedule, shooting on trains, 27 live musical numbers (all done live, no playback) and we made a really good soundtrack it was all production dialog with no ADR.

Q: Did you have any formal training?

A: I didn't have any formal training and I firmly believe that there is no formal institutional training that can really prepare you for this job. Even those who have gone to film school or received audio engineering degrees have their minds blown on the first day on set!

You really need to learn the job while on the job. What I DID have, which proved to be a huge benefit for me when starting out, was years and years on the set visiting my father working on movies. My father, Haskell Wexler, is a celebrated award winning director of photography - being on the set with him from the age of two, I learned so much about the art and creativity that goes into making a movie. I also learned the procedures, working on location, the importance of the personal and working relationships with the crew. All of these things have helped.

Q: How are production sound mixers compensated?

A: Everyone in production is paid an hourly wage. On a job that is being done under union contract, there is a minimum scale wage rate for the classification of work you do and a whole host of working conditions. As a union member you are free to negotiate and I have been successful negotiating 'Over Scale' much of the time.

Q: Is it important to live in LA?

A: If you asked this question 5 years ago I would have said yes. Today, I would first ask you if when you say "LA" do mean Los Angeles or Louisiana! With all the tax incentives and rebates in other states and the erosion of the Basic Agreement (West Coast contracts and pay rates), Los Angeles is becoming a ghost town in terms of production jobs. Television is still hanging in there but feature films have all but disappeared in Los Angeles

Q: If I was interested in pursuing a career as a Production Sound Mixer where might I start?

A: I would suggest trying to visit productions that are shooting, meet people who are doing the job and get a sense of what the work actually involves. You could also go to equipment rental houses, learn everything you can about the equipment currently being used in production and ask to assist in some way. Lastly spend some time with postproduction and arrange to visit a facility where you can meet sound editors and post mixers.

Q: Tell me something that most people don't know about your job.

A: I think there is still the myth that the sound that is recorded in production is not the sound that we hear in the theater or on tv. I have people come up to me on the set and ask me what I'm doing --- "Are you just recording everything so they know what the actors were saying?" or "Don't they do all the sound later in the studio?" They just have no idea. I would add that there is a lot that even the people in post don't know either. I've had post people come to the set and watched their jaws drop when they see what we are faced with in recording production sound; thankfully this usually translates into greater respect for the work we do.

Q: Have you ever had an intern, or mentored someone?

A: We have no formal system in the industry for internship or mentoring; this is unfortunate since it would be the best way to learn. However, I've served as chairman of our education committee at the Sound Local (union), taught classes at USC, UCLA, Art Center and AFI, founded jwsoundgroup.net a hugely successful online community for all those interested in sound for picture.

STUNTS

If you want to lead an adventurous life, sport a six-pack, have no fear, and don't mind that others get all of the credit for your hard work then becoming a stunt performer might be the perfect job for you.

From all of the crew I've spoken with, stunt performers are by far the tightest knit group. Maybe it's because they put their lives in the hands of each other daily, or because they like living on the edge and want to be around like-minded people. I don't know what it is but they take their work and fun very seriously.

First off, let's take in what famed stunt performer and coordinator Cal Johnson has to say about his world. Cal has worked on over 300 projects and if you just take a moment to look over his credits on IMDB you will immediately see that he is in high demand.

CAL JOHNSON

Stunt Coordinator

IMDB - The Walking Dead, We're the Millers, Ironman 3, Homeland, Stranger Things,
Fate of the Furious,

Q: Cal, would you explain the difference between a Stunt Performer and a Stunt Coordinator?

A: A stunt performer does the actual stunt, either as a nondescript stunt person or as a stunt double. The stunt coordinator choreographs and designs the stunt action. This means meeting with the director and coming up with action sequences, training actors, etc.

Q: What was your motivation for going into stunt work?

A: I saw *How the West was Won*, when I was in 5th grade. There was a man jumping off a train right into a cactus; I knew right then, I wanted to do that kind of thing.

Years later, after jumping off buildings and out of helicopters, crashing cars, and being set on fire myself I had the opportunity to have lunch with Loren Janes, one of Hollywood's most famous stuntmen and the stuntman I had watched jump from that moving train so many years before. I told him that he was the reason I wanted to be a stuntman and Janes said, "That's cool Cal, maybe one day you will hear that from someone who saw you!"

Q: Please explain the difference between working on a tv series vs. feature film?

A: Money! The stunts are similar, but the pay is far less for tv than a feature due to budgetary restraints.

Q: What are some of the most important skills someone would need to be a Stunt Coordinator?

A: It's quite a list and goes something like this:

> *Management expertise, creative problem solver, very detail oriented, knowledgeable of camera angles, action, ability to communicate with actors and directors tactfully, and how to fit everything nicely into a sometimes unrealistic budget.*

Q: Are there schools for stunt performers?

A: There are some, but nothing that is really reputable for our business. Learning as an apprentice is the best option out there.

Q: Cal, you were a stunt driver in the film *Need for Speed*. How do you keep pushing the limits of driving enough to engage an audience that has come to expect super-reality?

A: The biggest change is technology, which has helped stunts in general, but we still like to do the stunts practically when possible.

Sliding real cars at speed, crashing and flipping cars, safely. That only comes from years of experience and planning with a multitude of professionals involved.

On the technology side we often blend live action with technology. There are shots where you just have to use and the film business is moving quickly into the digital world, as I'm sure you already know. Most of the big budget projects are over half CGI these days, and many of the smaller budget ones as well.

Q: How do you typically get hired, do you have an agent, or manager?

A: I have 2 agents for commercials, but my tv and feature work is primarily from word of mouth, past relationships, or personally beating the bushes looking for jobs. For all my hard work these past 20 + years, I'm fortunate to be established as one of the top stunt coordinators in the South.

Q: How are you compensated, and are there residual royalties?

A: I usually get a daily or weekly rate, and yes we do receive residuals on the projects we work.

Q: Tell me something that most people don't know about Cal Johnson besides the fact that you probably have a bunch of well-healed fractures.

A: I love to cook and have been doing it since I was 10, when my mom got tired of baking me cookies and cakes all the time. She said, "If you want them so much, learn how to bake yourself," so I did.

Q: You've worked on over 300 projects; do you have a favorite?

A: Oh, gosh, that's like trying to pick your favorite candy bar. There have been many that stick out, but all, in some way or the other, have been fun. I have a dream job!

To be able to get up everyday and go to a job that you have wanted to do since you were a kid, and actually enjoy being there every moment, well, it doesn't get any better than that. I work with many of my best friends, get to hang out with some great actors, who have become close friends as well, and have a lot of fun creating action that will live eternally on film. What a great legacy.

Q: What is the most challenging part of your job?

A: Finding enough hours in the day to get everything done! Most days, I'm coordinating or working on multiple projects in different locations, hiring a multitude of people for each particular project, and then finding time for my girlfriend, getting my personal things done, while trying to find a little "Cal" time!

Q: Have you ever had an intern, or mentored someone?

A: I have had several assistants before, some good, some not so good. It's amazing sometimes how you try and give someone one hell of an opportunity that a majority of people in this business would kill for, and they just toss it away, while others, take it and run with it and do a great job.

Q: What's your best advice for someone entering your field?

A: Train, train, and train some more. Be patient, polite, never lie about your abilities, hustle and learn, network, and most importantly, pay it forward. Help out others because especially in our business what you put out there will come back to you.

Now that Cal Johnson has shed some light on the job of a stunt performer; let's hear from Rick Avery. Rick has over 365 film credits to his name and still found time to answers my questions. One thing you might notice is that Rick likes to work on epic high-energy projects.

RICK AVERY

Stuntman

IMDB - Titanic, Gangster Squad, Men in Black, The Dark Knight, Hands of Stone, and over 300 other films

Q: Rick, How did you break into the stunt business?

A: It took awhile and in the end it was just a stroke of luck. I trained hard for stunts and tried unsuccessfully for four years to get my SAG card. I was living in Santa Barbara and, commuting. At that time I owned a couple of Karate schools and decided to become a policeman in Santa Barbara instead after failing to make it as a stuntman.

I hustled Hal Needham on the set of *The End* and he was gracious enough to allow me to work on the movie. Hal loved cops and noticed me working on my motorcycle directing traffic for the movie. He called me over and asked if I wanted to be in a scene leading a funeral procession on my police motorcycle.

I did and after the scene Hal invited me to join the Stunts Unlimited team. He said " Kid, I like you, and I will be happy to introduce you to all the stuntmen pictured on that wall over there". He continued, " You have to go out and ride motocross with them, golf, train and get to know everybody, but I won't stand for a fence walker Rick. For me to do this you'll have to quit the police force sell your schools and your house and then move your family to Los Angeles.

There is no half way in this business". I thanked him and said I would think about it; then left. I was being offered a dream job delivered on the Needham platter, but I got scared and turned it down.

After four years on the force, I met John Travolta on a call and eventually became his personal bodyguard and Head of Security at his ranch. One night I was watching Hal Needham jump from a plane to a horse and I mentioned that's what I wanted to do to John's housekeeper. John found out I wanted to be a stuntman and put me on his next movie *Blow Out*. I doubled, and coordinated him for the next ten years.

Thanks to God I got a second chance to become a stuntman and didn't mess it up!

Q: Do you have a specialty like stunt driver, fire, or falls?

A: I came into this business as a fight professional but my mentor Alan Gibbs felt a stuntman should know as many skills as possible to stay busy and relevant in the business. I am not a high fall specialist; 55 feet was my max, and I hated that but I've done a lot of full burns, rappels, fights, ratchets, stair falls and all the rest, however you might say that driving is my specialty.

Q: What is a Stunt Coordinator?

A: A stunt coordinator is the gaffer or boss. He gets the script, breaks down the budget, and decides on equipment and personnel needed. He then meets with the director to see his vision for each stunt and then supervise that stunt so it is executed safely. The stunt coordinator hires the stuntmen/women keeping in mind their talent and experience. A seasoned coordinator will know all of the stunt folks presently active with the best abilities so the vision can be transferred to film. Many times the stunt coordinator is relied upon to set up the cameras and angles that would best sell the stunt on film.

Q: Would you tell me about your personal daily training routine?

A: I try never to be out of shape. When you go to the set they might want you to climb the tree before you fall out of it. My routine has changed over the years but I try to do cardio as well as light weight training. I do lots of sit-ups and pushups as well as an abbreviated form of P90x.

Presently, I also train 5 days a week as an amateur boxer in the USA boxing Masters division and have a couple of fights under my belt.

Q: Most people (not in the film business) think that Stuntmen are somewhat crazy for putting themselves at risk. Would you talk a little bit about safety and stunt preparation?

A: Well most people put themselves at risk just driving to work everyday and tens of thousands are killed annually. Research shows that we are born with what has been identified as "the risk gene". It can be a curse and a blessing. All extreme athletes have this gene. A curse because you constantly need to excel or compete... a blessing because you do Actually, by the time the stunt is performed, we have rehearsed it as much as needed to make it safe. In some respects the bigger the stunt the safer it is.

Murphy's law rules, "If it can go wrong, it will go wrong". I keep that in mind for every stunt, so all the bases are covered. For the little seen film *Blues Brothers 2000* I created, coordinated and performed in the biggest car wreck in history, where we jumped, rolled and crashed 54 cars in a sequence that is listed in the Guinness film book. I planned that stunt for 3 months with John Landis the director who also did the original *Blues Brothers*. He realized after we started production that the audience would want a big car sequence like in the original movie. He would come into my office every few days starting with a five-car pile-up finally ending with 54.

Most people now a days that see it, think it is CGI. It's not; a stuntman was driving each car We would crash 5 to10 at a time, get everybody out of the cars and start again. The whole sequence took only 2 days to shoot as Landis set 10 cameras and rolled the same 10 every time we yelled "action".

Q: I know that all days are different, but would you tell me about a typical day at the office (during production)?

A: I have been stunt doubling for Robert De Niro on his last few movies. My last one I got called to coordinate and second unit direct. The movie was called *Hands of Stone*. The producer and director asked me to come to Panama to do a "little" boxing movie. This movie was not little, and had more than boxing in it. Over 10,000 extras, riots, explosions, stair falls, high falls, foot chases, never mind multiple re-enactments of major historic boxing matches.

A typical day would involve going to the gym to teach and choreograph the fights with Usher, who plays Sugar Ray Leonard, and Edgar Ramirez, who plays Roberto Duran. In Panama the days are extremely hot, and humid. After the morning work, we would have location scouts and production meetings. I would go over all of the action with the director, and all of the department heads. Once production started we would go for 12 hours a day or more. I only had maybe 5 days off in four and a half months.

Q: Are Stuntmen paid well?

A: Stuntmen are paid as actors are. We are members of The Screen Actors Guild and ACTRA. For that reason we have minimums that are paid by production. Stuntmen will come in to sign either a daily or weekly stunt contract.

Then if the stunt deserves additional compensation, the coordinator will add a "stunt adjustment" or "stunt bump" to the contract. The stunt adjustment varies and depends on the coordinators experience, budget and how many times the stuntman had to do it. Add overtime to this and it is a good days work. Stunt Coordinators usually will get more than the minimums if they have a resume to back it up. Some of us are also in the directors Guild so we will also get compensated if we second unit direct. Yes there are residuals.

Q: Tell me about the best time you've ever had working on a film.

A: My best time was on *Batman Begins*. I made a lot of new friends on that one. I have done four Batman movies and loved them all. One night Chris Nolan the director called me over on the radio. I thought I was in trouble but he said that one of the actors he hired couldn't drive the police car with all the cameras and lights on it while doing dialogue so he had me take the actor's place. I felt really bad for the guy. So I got a couple of lines and close-ups in the movie. On *Batman Returns*, we did a huge 30-person ratchet when the penguin explodes the dance floor. On *Batman Begins*, *Batman the Dark Knight* and *Dark Knight Rises*, I was usually the lead in the car chases as well as driving other crash vehicles.

Q: I've noticed that many Stunt people are Martial Artists ...Why is this?

A: It was not that way when I started in 1979. Now Martial Arts are popular in many shapes and styles. MMA is very popular so you will find stunt folks all getting some basics under their belts so if they are asked to do a kick or martial arts fight, they will at least have a base to start from. You don't want to show up on a set, especially if you are doubling an actor and find that he does kicks better than you do.

Q: Tell me something that most people don't know about Rick Avery.

A: I have been a hard worker all my life. I have always had a couple of professions. I work seven days a week. I have been a stuntman for 35 years but I have also been a commercial pilot for the same amount of time. For the last 11 years I have been a helicopter pilot and aerial coordinator in addition to the stunts and directing. I have almost 6,000 hours combined with over 4,000 of them in helicopters.

So tomorrow I might be doing a car chase, and the next day I might be chasing the cars with my helicopter. Only now are my flying skills being sought out on commercials, movie and television production. Last year I worked for Guardian Helicopters fighting fires. I still work for Group 3 Aviation as a line pilot and instructor, and I am chief pilot at National Helicopters whose helicopters were used on the original Batman tv. Series.

Q: What might be the best advice you could give a young person who wants to be successful as a stunt person?

A: Never take no for an answer. Spend all day everyday meeting stunt folks, and coordinators. Refine your skills, for your body is your tool. Train every day on those skills so when you are asked to finally perform, you excel. Over a period of years, most people will know your name and your ability if you follow this advice.

PROPERTY MASTER

I need a clock from the early 1600's and a 41 inch hotdog", says the director.

'Not a problem, give me about 20 minutes', answers the Property Master who then gives their assistant instruction and sends them on their way.

All in a day's work for the person that's in charge of all of the props you see in a film. Props can include anything an actor touches, or food, or … a clock from the 1600's. The Property Master finds them and then manages where they go.

I don't remember exactly how I found Francois, but I love his work, especially on *Amelie*. When I first contacted him, he asked if he might send me his answers in French, his native language. I hope this translation agrees with him!

FRANCOIS BORGEAUD
Property Master

IMDB - Taken, Grace of Monaco, Hugo, Renegades

Q: Francois, as a Property Master what are your responsibilities?

A: It's hard to explain exactly what I do because it is so varied but to summarize, I'm in charge of everything that happens in the hands of the actors, as well as everything they handle during filming (cigarettes, luggage, food).

The property master also has assistants, buyers (props buyer) and tray props (stand by prop crew). These people work closely with the design department, but are freelance and independent. In France, the Property Master is part of the art department and which takes care accessories and decorations once shooting starts.

Q: How would you typically start a project?

A: In preproduction, I read the script like a book so I can fully understand the characters, the atmosphere and such. Then I read it a second time and look for places that would have direct relations, for example: "he writes a letter", "smokes a cigarette", "takes out his wallet". There also less obvious things such as "walking through the kitchen of a large restaurant", " a car passes", etc. One a third reading I will make notes of all of the possible accessories that will be required to make the scene realistic.

Q: Did you have special training for your job?

A: I think the best course is to work directly with a Property Master. I know of no schools (at least in France) that can properly train someone in the profession of prop handling. There are courses that explain the business by embracing the trades of film decoration in general, and these can be a helpful, but nothing beats learning from someone in the field.

Q: What types of skills are required in your profession?

A: First and foremost you must be resourceful. It is true that we take care of everything that happens in the hands of the actors, but it is also the last minute tinkering to facilitate the crew, for example oiling a squeaky door or moving a table to avoid a reflection that bothers the camera. It's always these kinds of small tweaks that we must find, invent, imagine and fix.

You must also be a great observer because apart from accessories fittings throughout the shoot, you need to be in tune with what's going on around you and anticipate everything. For example on a recent project an actress had to walk through a door with two locks. I noticed on the first rehearsal that she had difficulty manipulating them because of the bags she was carrying. I saw this and quickly I covered the locks so she would just pretend to unlock them.

Q: How is a Master Property compensated?

A: In France the labor rate in 2017 was € 1,320 for a 39 hour week.

Q: Is there a logical career path to become a Property Master?

A: It is best to start by becoming a trainee with the props department, move up to an assistant position and finally do small projects as a leader under the guidance of a property master. There is no manual!

Q: Do you have some advice for a young person that would like to be a Property Master?

A: To do this job, like any in the film business, it is very important to be curious and observant on the set. You should also do this in your everyday life because it directly relates to when you need to transcribe a script. It is the little details that help the viewer believe what they are seeing. It is the breadcrumbs on the table at dinner, or the rings left by a cup of coffee that has been moved.

The most important thing to me is to have fun doing my job because cinema is a medium that can be stressful in in our movie set world.

Q: How do you get hired?

A: For me it works only by word of mouth; either because I have already worked with a production manager, a director, an assistant or because my name has been circulated, "we've heard about you". This is also what makes me stay on top of my profession and not rest on my laurels. I never take this job for granted and continue to improve myself over and over.

PRODUCTION ASSISTANT

In the world of film production, there are few intern or apprentice opportunities. Insurance, unions and other factors keep them from participating in most cases even though most if not all of the key crew positions would like to foster the growth of the traditional methods of filmmaking.

In the film industry, Production Assistant is the entry-level position and the starting place for many. Most departments in film have production assistants that do the running around to pick up materials, hold cables, move stuff around the set, etc.

Earlier, I introduced Samuel Alder as a location scout, but he is back again and this time as a production assistant. Sam is the perfect illustration a crewmember that wears many hats!

SAMUEL ADLER

Production Assistant

IMDB - Hall Pass, Orange is the New Black, The Watch, Due Date

Q: Sam, so what would you do as a PA on a film, or tv production?

A: PAs do the odd jobs for whatever department they are hired to work in. Rather it be on set, the production office, camera department, locations, or writers office. It's the perfect job to break into the industry as a non-union member and work your way up.

The PAs job might entail simply ordering lunch for the office (Don't mess this up!), maintaining office supplies, making photo copies of scripts, answering phones, ordering supplies, controlling access to set during takes, directing extras on set, picking up actors from hotels and airports, organizing paperwork.

Oh, and the infamous late night FedEx drop off when you quickly learn where to find the last delivery pick up in your city. This knowledge is worth its weight in PA gold. The phrase "Lets put my college education to good use" tends to be uttered often as a PA.

So, it's a long random list of not so glamorous duties, but everyone on the show knows that the PAs are the hardest working people on the show making the lowest amount of money. Being a PA is a great way to show people just how diligent and hard working you are. You would be surprised how many people leave or get fired because they don't see the big picture and never get passed the PA stage.

Q: Do you work long hours?

A: The film industry is well known for working long hours and the standard is a 12-hour day with a half-hour lunch. You work until you are sent home… whenever that is.

It's not uncommon to work 16-18 hour days even as a PA, and yes, you do get overtime. Over all you should expect to work a minimum of 60 hours a week and as high as 80. My personal best is 90 hours in a single week.

Q: What's the standard pay scale for a PA?

A: PAs generally get the same pay scale regardless of responsibility. There are always productions that are willing to pay you more and some that are cheap and want to pay less. Expect $125 to $150 for a 12-hour day not including over time. Reality tv will pay a bit less, and film and episodic pay about the same. Commercials pay the most at around $200 a day, but commercials only last a day or two.

If you're a Key Set PA or Paperwork PA chances are you may get paid a bit more. It's all up to the show and if your boss is willing to push for it. If someone wants to pay you anything below $100 for a 12-hour day, *"worker be warned."* It's a low-budget show and you may just want to take the job for the experience.

Q: Samuel, what's the best time you've ever had working on a film?

A: For me it's when I arrive before the sun is up and get everything ready on set. You can hear the trucks and generators humming, the smell of breakfast being prepared for the crew, and if you take a moment to stop and watch the sun rise over basecamp (staging area) you begin to feel thankful that you have the privilege to do what you love with some very talented and passionate people…then all hell breaks loose on the radio and you snap back into reality!

Q: What type of education did you have, and did it prepare you for feature film work?

A: I am technically a college drop out, but I like to say I just spent a ton of money on schooling and didn't want to spend anymore. So I left and looked for ways to make money in the film world. I studied Digital Media Production but I've never used it. I would say the best use of my education was the five years spent at Home Depot. I even got hired once because I mentioned it in the interview and they wanted someone handy.

Being able to trouble shoot problems, work around construction materials, and deal with the crazy public have given me the best experience. The second part would be the Civil Air Patrol (Aux of the USAF) I was involved with when I was in my teens. Film crews are much like the military. There's a chain of command and lots of "hurry up and wait" moments.

Q: Is the job of a PA a stepping-stone?

A: The PA position is entry level and doesn't pay very well compared to what you will be making in the future. You should have fun and explore working in different departments. Then figure out where you want to work in the industry and move in that direction.

UNIT STILLS PHOTOGRAPHER

Do you ever wonder where all of the beautiful production stills used in the marketing of a film come from? Yes, there are people dedicated to capturing these images and I hear that it's a wonderful job! You get to travel, hang with the Actors and Actresses, interface with the crew and barely break a sweat … at least most of the time.

Men in Black, The Secret life of Walter Mitty, True Grit, Gangster Squad all have one thing in common, Mr. Wilson Webb.

WILSON WEBB
Unit Stills Photographer

Q: Wilson, please tell me about your job as a Unit Stills Photographer?

A: I am an On-Set Photographer and my job is to capture photos of the cast, to document the making of a film, and to help supply photographic props that might be used in the film. My job also might include what we call a 'Gallery Shoot', which is specifically for images to use for the main film poster, and for other advertising artwork.

Q: I've read that you got your start as an film electrician. How did that position evolve into Production Still Photographer?

A: Growing up, I always had a camera around, as my father was an amateur photographer. I went on to study filmmaking and photography in high school and then college. During my junior year at The Minneapolis College of Art and Design I worked on an alumni's film and I met local gaffer, David Meyers. He liked my work ethic and asked if I would be interested in joining his crew.

So, in my senior year I worked on a studio film and was also covertly sneaking photos on-set while working. This was years before cell-phones and I had a very compact film camera that allowed me to be low profile (as taking photos isn't really allowed by anyone but the set photographer). I continued to move up the chain to become a gaffer and eventually to DP, all the while working on side photo projects. It wasn't until The Coen Brothers *A Serious Man* that I started shooting stills as a full time job.

Q: Do you start with a list of photos you need to capture or is it more of a creative job?

A: It's really more creative, for the most part. Sometimes a studio will give you a head's up about what is important to them but more likely that they just trust that I will capture the vital images, as a big part of my job is to know what they need.

Q: Who would typically hire you?

A: The hiring can come form many different places but I would say that I have been fortunate enough to get a lot of work from directors, and from their referrals. I have also been hired from photo editors suggesting me to a production. When Joel and Ethan Coen suggest you to another director it's quite a door opener, to put it mildly.

Q: Is there a set pay scale for an On-Set Photographer?

A: For all union jobs there is a pay scale that is dependent on the overall budget, or tier, of the film. It's really just a minimum that the production company has to pay you - but that's just the beginning of the negotiation. We also are paid a rental rate for all of our personal photography gear.

Q: What is the most challenging part of fulfilling your role shooting stills?

A: Every project has a different set of challenges; sometimes it's the pressures of the location, or the interactions with actors, while sometimes it's the challenge of capturing the spirit of the film. Quite often it can be a challenge to find a good place to shoot from and to not be in anyone's way.

My job is ever changing, but that's the fun part! On *The Secret Life of Walter Mitty* I started a month before filming began, which is somewhat unusual. We needed to shoot fake film posters (they were planned to be used throughout the film but were ultimately cut) and to figure out all the photographic props needed for the film, as this particular story is about a photo editor, photography played an important role in the story line. If you see the film, there is one major prop photo of a thumb - that's the closest to stardom that I have come (as that photo is a self portrait)!

Q: Can someone make a nice living doing what you do?

A: I seemed to have done ok! The union has seen a lot of changes in the recent past and many photographers fear that our position will grow smaller as the people rely more on frame captures from the newer digital cameras but that route would really limit their visual options for marketing purposes.

Only time will tell but I will say that if this is what you desire to do, you should always keep your options open. Not only does that keep you flexible but it also forces you to perhaps learn about other aspects of photography and to be more educated in general, which will result in better work. I can't speak for photographers who just shoot tv, or smaller budgeted projects but at the level that I work it is possible to have a good career.

Q: Do you travel in your occupation?

A: Yes, there is a lot of travel, and that is just part of the job in our current times. It used to be that LA and New York were the main places where projects were filmed, but with the ever-changing tax incentives productions are using the entire world as their canvas. I do enjoy being in different places but it can be challenging especially if you have a family. The 'film crew' lifestyle is often compared to that of a traveling circus and it seems to be an appropriate analogy.

Q: Favorite job?

A: Thinking back *PAUL* was a lot of fun because the on-set mood was always great and all the crew were so easy going. *A Serious Man* was amazing, but I sure was nervous most of the time! *30 Minutes or Less* was also a blast because of the talent involved.

Another film was *The Secret Life of Walter Mitty* and I was very involved in producing the key prop photos, which was both gratifying and challenging. In the end it's the relationships that I have made through the years and the work that comes from those collaborations that makes it all worth while to me.

Q: Do you work on other types of productions besides feature films?

A: Sometimes I still DP commercial projects and I also work on personal assignments, but it's tough since my schedule is always changing. I like to keep busy.

Q: What advice would you give a young person aspiring to have a job like yours?

A: Shoot as much as possible; build your portfolio and your work experience doing whatever you can at first. Don't turn down any job unless the conditions are dreadfully bad. Many people start on freebies and slowly work their way up.

I would add that studying all types of photography is helpful (past and present), never stop learning. Use all the resources at your disposal and many of them are free; the Internet, the library, museums, etc. Don't allow yourself to be limited to learning about any one style as all influences are helpful and will lead you to your own unique vision.

Lastly, networking and getting to know the people that make up the film community is vital It may appear quite daunting looking in from the outside but the film community is really relatively small. One important thing that I try to stress to people who want to work at any role in this field is that there is no one path that everyone follows, so allow yourself to find your own way.

Q: Do you ever use traditional film or has the industry transitioned 100% to digital?

A: Most set photographers shoot little to no film these days. The studios have fewer tools to process film and adapted to 100 % digital. I try to shoot as much film as possible because it's beautiful, has amazing texture and is historic. Some directors I work with agree and on those projects I shoot as much as possible in different formats.

Q: Wilson, would you mind sharing a story, or situation you've experienced with a director, or Actor where the shoot didn't go as expected?

A: The process of filmmaking is about adapting to changes and situations constantly. It can be a $250MM film or a $16MM film and the challenges seem to be very similar, with the only difference being the size of the 'Stars' trailer!

On one recent film the director didn't feel like the scene was going anywhere so he had the actors do it without any dialogue. It was really fun to watch. Weather, locations, and actors are just a small part of our day to day, and we have top stay sharp and be ready to find a solution to the next problem that will surely creep up…because it's probably only minutes away!

Q: In most professional photography you would own the images you shoot, is this also the case for you?

A: Yes, things are different for 'On Set Photographers' because of the actor clearances and the nature of photo manipulation. The studio owns all the rights to any image taken on set. The actors, or their management approve all of the images taken during the filming process, so they are comfortable with how they are represented. Once the studio releases any image we also have the right to use them for our own representation, however we can never sell them.

Q: Any other last comments?

A: A lot of my job is about interpersonal communications and conducting myself in a professional way that allows the actors and other film crews to feel comfortable about my presence. Sometimes knowing where NOT to be is one of the most important skills that we can have.

A set is often a crazy, cramped place and the last thing that you want is to be in anyone's way. You always have to remember that the on-set photographer is one of very few jobs on set that does not require your presence to be there in order for the film to get made. Don't forget that every actor, and every film crew is different and it's an ongoing learning process.

ACCOUNTING

So who takes care of the money? If I had invested $200 million into a film, I'd sure want to know how the funds are being spent!

The people that manage all the money in a production are called 'Production Accountants' and they're responsible for making sure the production companies, and crew are paid. The production accountants on large projects have assistants that take care of the payroll, and accounts receivable/payable leaving time for the accountants to watch the bigger picture.

Remember earlier I mentioned how many crewmembers juggle multiple jobs? Well, here we are again with Samuel Adler (location manager/accounting) ; man of many talents. I couldn't help but ask Sam a few questions about other areas of the business because he has seen so much. This is short and sweet!

SAMUEL ADLER

Accounting

IMDB - Hall Pass, Orange is the New Black, The Watch, Due Date

Q: Tell me about your job as an accounting clerk ... how did it start?

A: Ha! I always laugh at this question. Well it was an odd answer to prayer. After working on one film I realized I was terrible at paper work as most production people are (the reason we work in production), and thought if I had the opportunity to become proficient in that area I would do so. That was my prayer at least…

A few months later I was helping out a production accountant set up his office for a few days and he asked me if I wanted to stay and be his clerk. The rest, as they say is history.

Q: What type of skill set would I need for a position in production accounting?

A: Just bring a positive attitude, good brain, great analytical skills, ability and desire to focus on details. You have to be okay with working in an office with paperwork all day so if you want to work on set, don't go into accounting. No accounting degree is needed…everything is a trade / craft so its all hands on training. I would add that knowing how to use Excel comes in handy…

Q: What's your day look like as an accounting clerk?

A: Sorting the inbox(s) and delivery of items to different people. Making coffee for the boss (putting that college education to good use). Date stamping, lots of filing, opening and sorting mail. Being a point person to sign in and out purchase orders. That's a highly important task and you get connected with lots of people from the entire show. Delivering paychecks which means everyone is happy to see you. The list goes on with small details.

FILM EDITOR

Have you ever edited a family vacation video and wondered why it just didn't look professional? Taking that 4 hours of random video you shot and cutting it into a coherent 10 minute masterpiece is not only daunting, it can seem impossible for most of us. That's unless you are one of a handful of master film editors. They can take miles of film footage and cut it together in such a way that the story gets told, the director is happy, the studios are happy, the producers are happy, and ok… everybody is happy!

If everything goes right in the edit suite most of us mere mortals will never even think about the process of film editing, much less the disaster the film may have become had it not been for their thoughtful creative, and tireless attention to detail.

While there are film editors that work primarily in the episodic tv world, there are others that take on longer form feature films. One such person is Mark Sanger who won an Oscar for his work on *Gravity*. In watching the film again I noticed his deep understanding of where the camera was in relation to the cast, and viewer. He does this while concurrently thinking about the action, the story, and the desired emotional response for every scene.

Photo Courtesy of Ross Grieve

MARK SANGER

Film Editor

IMDB – Gravity (Oscar Winner), The Mummy, and Jungle Book: Origins, Last Knights

Q: Mark, first off I'd like to offer my congratulations for winning the 'Oscar' for your editing of *Gravity*. Tell me a little about your job.

A: All films evolve as they are made. Nothing is committed to film exactly as the director had envisioned. I see the role of the editor as an aid to the director in a way that best serves both the director's original vision and the evolving story. In the case of something as technically ambitious as *Gravity* it is important to always be serving the story rather than the phantasmagoria.

Q: An important skill needed to become a successful film editor?

A: An understanding of the political landscape on any given project and an ability to adapt to that landscape in order to gauge the best way to tell the story.

The making of any film is a political process and this can either be a pleasure to negotiate, or a diplomatic quagmire, but without the ability to wade through the quagmire, the story will never be told to its best advantage.

Q: At what point are you brought in on a film?

A: Traditionally an editor is brought on perhaps two weeks before shooting begins, but with the advent of pre-visualization storyboarding, the process has evolved somewhat in the past decade. The editor is sometimes required much earlier than this, as believe it or not, nowadays some editorial decisions need to have been made prior to commencement of shooting.

Q: Would you tell my readers what was running through your head in the moments before they announced 'Mark Sanger' as an Oscar winner for your work on *Gravity*?

A: To be honest with you I was convinced that my friend Chris Rouse had won for *Captain Phillips*. All the other nominees had done astounding work and as clichéd as it sounds, I was truly privileged to be named among them. However Chris had won the ACE award a few weeks earlier and I thought I saw a trend. So when they announced that 'Gravity' had won, I had not even prepared a speech.

The next thirty minutes was a strange whirlwind of press and photographs, and then I found myself and sat back next to my wife again with an Academy Award. It was all quite surreal

Q: Did you know while you were editing *Gravity* that this might be 'the one'?

A: None of us (editors) choose our projects based upon which are more likely to win accolades, however anything Alfonso Cuaron creates is likely to be interesting to say the least. It was not until four years after we began the project that we had any suspicion that audiences would engage with the film. We were all quite immersed in the process of making it and I for one was quite focused on the detail and could no longer see the bigger picture.

After the film premiered at the Venice Film Festival I was pleasantly surprised to find that people were connecting with it the way they have. It meant that the combined efforts of the cast and crew were shining through.

Q: What types of technical challenges were you faced with on 'Gravity', i.e.: green screen, new technologies that you had not used before?

A: The primary challenge was to work out exactly how we would make a complex film. Everything about the process was different and therefore brought its own unique set of challenges. We were a team of professionals who shared not only knowledge of our own departments, but also a common knowledge of each other's. That is what made *Gravity* the film experience that it is...collaboration.

Q: Might you recall some of the stepping-stones that brought you to where you are today?

A: I took every full advantage of every opportunity that was offered to me. I started as a runner on a BBC tv show, switching traffic lights on and off to stop the public driving through shot during a take. I then worked in pretty much every department in order to keep working and to maintain a broad base of experience.

I worked in the art, special effects, location and then production departments before finally getting my first editorial break as a runner on a James Bond film. I regard each of these departments, and each film that followed, as stepping-stones because the truth is that none of us ever stop learning.

Q: Is there a pay scale for a film editor?

A: There are pay scales if you are in the US union but beyond that it really comes down to circumstance. If a large production really wants a specific editor they may be prepared to pay more money, however as much as we need to pay our bills, most editors will reduce their rates if the script and team could be interesting to work with.

Q: What was the most challenging part of editing *Gravity* in terms of creating 'the look' that Alfonso wanted?

A: Alfonso Cuaron, who sees the film very clearly in his head from inception, dictated the editorial style. The greatest challenge for me as co-editor was keeping up with the speed of his creative ideas as they evolved and translating those to the screen in a way that did them justice.

Q: Who are some of the other people you interact with during the editing of a film?

A: I interact with as many of the crew as possible and as often as I can. However, on a daily-to-day basis it is more likely that an editor will be primarily concerned with the director and the editorial team.

Q: I understand that most days are different but would you tell me about a typical day at work?

A: During the shoot, the first job of the day is to assess the dailies and discuss the plan for their inclusion, as well as how they will affect the tone and structure of the scene and story overall.

During post it is initially about getting as much time as possible with the director to refine this process. Invariably we are editing the film in some fashion from day one shoot to the last day of the sound mix, even to the point where we make picture changes on the stage. Beyond this framework I think it is fair to say that this no such thing as typical day in editorial.

Q: Career advice?

A: Meet as many people in the industry as you can. Work in as many departments as possible, as hard and enthusiastically as you can, all the time with the secret motive of establishing a broad education and remembering there is always the prospect of grabbing a job as editorial trainee somewhere along the line.

Q: What was the best time you've ever had working on a film?

A: I was lucky enough to be hired as an assistant editor on three James Bond films. Receiving and prepping the dailies from the multiple units each day was a true honor and pure fun. It was a daily adrenaline rush and I was privileged to be working not only with some of my personal industry heroes but also with others who have become some of my closest friends.

Q: What type of education did you have, and did it prepare you for editing feature films?

A: I had a regular schooling in the UK and never attended film school. I was keen to get my foot in the door as soon as I left school so I started knocking on doors immediately. My film education was with the many amazing crews I've had the pleasure to train under in those early years. But the truth is that my education never stops.

Q: Have you ever had an intern?

A: As a team we hire interns on every film. They are not only a crucial part of our working environment but as the years go by we all try to feed off their fresh enthusiasm!

I think that anyone who believes they cannot learn from fresh ideas, both technically and creatively is starving himself or herself of the very inspiration that started them in the industry in the first place.

Q: What does the future look like for film editorial as a career path?

A: There used to be an air of mystery as to what we do, which was both a blessing and a curse. The digital age has opened many possibilities for young filmmakers. When I was a boy, you had to have particular tools to edit film, which were hard to come by for newcomers. It's now a more accessible craft, which is exciting because it means more talented people have the opportunity to showcase their work than before.

However, just because people own some digital editing software does not necessarily make them an editor. Nevertheless it is very positive to see more and more people wanting to learn about a craft that had once been very mystical.

One of the busiest editors I know of is Jane Kass. Editing for television and series work is intense and requires a special type of person. Jane as you will read is a dedicated, creative, award-winning editor that tells it like it is. The hours are long, and the creativity is demanding on a show like *NCIS*, but she handles it all in stride like the seasoned professional she is.

JANE KASS
Film/TV Editor

IMDB - NCIS, Without a Trace, The Practice, Hit the Floor, Criminal Minds, Gone

Q: As the editor on a show like *Hostages,* what's your basic process Jane?

A: I receive all of the film shot the previous day and cut it together to make it seem like the people are actually having a conversations with each other! There might be many different takes of each setup and I have to determine which are the best line readings from each character.

I make all of the decisions about how the film is to be cut and then present it to the director or producer who will make the ultimate decisions. On *Hostages*, I was lucky to have producers who trust my work and knew that I'd deliver a cut that was very close to what they had envisioned so they made very few changes in what I had originally put together.

Q: What are some of the differences between what you do as a Television series editor and a feature film editor?

A: In tv, we receive much more film in a shorter amount of time. We have tighter deadlines and don't have the luxury of working scenes over and over for days on end until everyone is satisfied. When I working as an assistant on features, I worked with an editor who told me that he cut about 250 feet of film a day, which translates to about two and a half minutes a day.

In television we edit between 6 and 8 minutes each day. This includes putting in sound effects and music and delivering a completely scored show. This is only possible because we work in the digital world. In features, they hire a music editor to create a temp score before they deliver the picture to the producers; something that a tv production cannot afford.

Q: What do you consider the most important skills for an editor?

A: Know how to make a computer sing! There are no tv shows or features that are edited on film anymore and they don't even release movies in the theatres on film. The next most important skill is to be detail oriented. An editors job starts with looking at all of the dailies to check for differences in takes as far as performance, camera moves, little looks that characters might give, etc.

Many young people come right out of film school and think that because they know the computer and software that they can be great editors. This is not the case. I learned my craft by sitting behind experienced editors, watching very closely, asking questions and learning on the job. I watched how they made choices and where they were going next. They would know all of the film before they cut the first frame. That's how I was taught to cut.

Q: Are you typically hired because of your editing style, past experience, technical expertise, or geographic location?

A: All of the above. I have a lot of experience in procedural dramas like *NYPD Blue, Without a Trace, The Practice*, etc.

I am now working on a show that is completely away from my safe zone. It's a scripted show for VH1 that deals with a fictional dance team, similar to the *Laker Girls*. It has lots of music and lots of dance numbers. It's a big detour from what I am used to but good for me because I'm learning a completely different way to edit. The show has lots of quick cuts in the dance numbers but there's also an element of drama dealing with what goes behind the scenes of the dance team and the basketball team they dance for.

So to answer your question, I have a reputation but sometimes it stands in the way of getting jobs because I don't have experience editing certain genres. Hopefully, this show will open some new doors.

Q: Is there a specific pay scale for a tv editor and does it differ from film, or commercial work?

A: There is a union pay scale for editors but depending on where you work in tv it's usually a little higher than scale. Features are a completely different story.

Feature editors can earn anywhere from $5,000 to $20,000 a week depending on their status Some editors are attached to specific directors and those editors are the highest paid. Clint Eastwood, Martin Scorcese, Tim Burton, Steven Spielberg, all have one editor they always work with and sometimes the editors are even kept on retainer in between projects.

In tv, that doesn't happen. A director might have an editor that he/she always works with but budgets in tv are not as high as features, therefore, tv editors don't earn anywhere near what feature editors can demand.

Q: Do you primarily work for a production company or as a sub-contractor?

A: I work wherever I can get a job, however more than half of my career has been at Warner Bros. I started there as an apprentice and learned my craft. It used to be that the heads of postproduction for the studios would hire the editors and the assistant editors. That doesn't happen anymore. You have to know the producers of the projects to get an interview or have a relationship with them in order to get hired. I have that relationship with the wonderful people at Bruckheimer tv. I have worked with them on and off for the past ten years.

Q: What was the most challenging project you've worked on?

A: Actually, the show I am currently working is the most challenging. Because of all the music and dance numbers and the tremendous amount of footage to go through. Before I started this job, I watched the first season's episodes over and over in order to get a feel for what the producers wanted in the dance numbers. I examined how cutty they wanted them to be and how they featured the main characters of the show. When I finally got dailies on my first dance number, it was really fun to edit the dance. It came out great if I do say so myself.

Q: Do you have some advice for an aspiring editor?

A: Know storytelling. If you can't tell a story, then you might as well forget about editing. Next thing I would say is really knowing your editing system inside and out. The way to get into this business today is to really be exceptional in this area.

I suppose the last and maybe most important piece is learning to edit music and sfx because the business is changing and many of these responsibilities that have been done by others in the past will soon to be yours.

Q: What was the best time you've ever had working on a project?

A: I absolutely loved working on *The Practice* for David E. Kelley as well as *Hostages* for Bruckheimer tv. *The Practice* was like working with one big family. Everyone knew each other and usually the production crew doesn't know anyone in Post Production, but because we were all in the same building and there were so many get-togethers such as our annual Halloween Costume Contest. Plus, they were very kind and generous to us as far as supplying lunches, and other amenities. The directors would bring in a coffee truck at the end of their episodes, and sometimes David would send in the In 'N Out' Burger truck.

On *Hostages*, we were a tighter knit group because the production was in N.Y. and the writers and Post were in L.A. The two showrunners, Jeffrey Nachmanoff and Rick Eid, were the two nicest guys you could possibly work for. They trusted their editors and knew that we would execute their notes correctly and in a timely manner. They weren't ones who would sit in the room with us for 12 hours a day and watch every little move we made. It was just a very pleasant work environment.

Q: What type of education did you have, and how well did it prepare your job?

A: I graduated from UCLA with a B.A. in Film and Television. I learned a lot but it was mostly 'on the job' training that prepared be for the editorial world. Today, I would say that a college education is crucial in entering this field. First of all, college will prepare someone for the world of business, whatever area a person may choose. Secondly, a film student today will learn how to use the tools of our trade.

Q: Have you ever mentored someone?

A: I try to mentor all of my assistants and help them get ready to be editors. I'll have them sit in the room with me while I am editing and explain why I make the cuts that I do and how to figure out problematic scenes. Most of my assistants have moved on to become very successful editors in their own right.

Q: What should the world know about Jane Kass?

A: I love what I do and I do it well. I have always been enamored with the film business and have been involved in it since I was a little girl because my father was in the distribution of films. He died suddenly when he was only 57 and didn't really get to see me achieve what I have in this business, including winning the American Cinema editors Award for an episode of *NYPD Blue*. I know he's aware of what I've accomplished, but it would have been nice to have him here to see it.

ANIMATION

We live in an animated world made up of digital characters, avatars, tablets, technology and Nano-second innovation chains. It's no wonder that this has spilled into the film world; it's all part of the process. I worry that some of my very best friends will lose their eyesight prematurely because they stare endlessly at computer screens making *minute* adjustments to an image, or mathematic calculations that other humans wouldn't notice anyway.

I purposefully interviewed several people in this segment of the film business because the growth is so impressive. You simply can't watch a film today that doesn't have at least a few digital efx shots and there appears to be a job to fit just about every personality type, intellectual curiosity, and creative discipline.

Today the industry is changing so quickly with regards to animation, virtual reality, and 3D that very soon you will see studios producing commercially viable films with fully digitally created actors and actresses. They will be built on digital workstations, which will translate into thousands of jobs for designers, engineers, artists, riggers, and every imaginable position related to digital creation, and it's coming fast!

Collectively, the following people I interviewed represent just about every major film release of the last decade including all of the blockbusters.

Graduating from Teesside University in 2009, Manjoe worked his way up the production pipeline, from runner, matchmover to animator. He has experience as a character animator at companies such as Framestore, Blue Zoo, and Pixomondo working on both feature films, and tv productions.

MANJOE CHAN
Animator and Matchmove Artist

IMDB - Gravity, Harry Potter, Ironman 3, Guardians of the Galaxy, Spider-Man: Homecoming, Thor: Ragnarok

Q: You're an amazing Animator Manjoe, would you tell me about your job?

A: Thank you Michael, as an animator, we take rigged assets, which is basically a 3d model with a virtual skeleton, transforming it into a puppet of sorts. This could either be a character (such as *Iron Man*), or a vehicle, and we make it move according to our supervisors brief. In Iron Man 3, I was given the Iron Man character and animated it against live action plates.

Q: Would you explain the difference between an Animator and a Matchmove Artist?

A: A 'Matchmove' artist is typically the first step of a postproduction pipeline. Matchmove artists have a much more technical job, solving camera moves to match live action plates allowing the rest of the artists and technicians to in the pipeline to work in 3D against the plate. Animators then take this camera, the original live action footage, and animate whatever they need to animate within the shot and it all lines up. This is a massive simplification of the process, in *Gravity*, the pipeline was much more complex.

Q: At what point in production do you get involved?

A: There is a lot of overlapping in the vfx pipeline of any film and sometimes animators are brought on early to do testing, but these always follow modeling and rigging; otherwise we have nothing to animate. Once they have filmed the live action plates, it goes through tracking and animation can get inserted into the process.

Q: Would you tell me about your work on the film *Gravity*?

A: For anyone that's seen any of the *Gravity* vfx breakdowns, you will know that 90% of what you see on screen was CG, and for the exterior shots, only the faces within the helmets were real. So, taking what they filmed on set, for the animators to be able to animate the body and for it to appear connected to the head, the trackers have to work their magic. Trackers basically had to track the camera, and also the helmet, making sure the relationship between the two were completely accurate, allowing the animators to manipulate the scene as they pleased, but still keeping the essence of what was originally shot in tact.

Q: Do you work as a sub contractor, or as an employee for a visual effects company?

A: I work as an employee on a fixed term contract. Compared to freelancing, it is much more secure, but the rate of pay is a bit lower.

Q: Tell me something that most people don't know about the role of an animator on a big budget production?

A: What you seen on screen, is never the first version; it's more like the 100th!

Q: What is the most challenging part of your job?

A: Art is very subjective, so to be able to match the director's vision is the hardest part.

Q: Advice for an aspiring Animator?

A: Practice, practice, practice and work hard. Never hold back and continue to push yourself; you should be your own biggest critic.

Boris Plateau lives in Montreal, Canada and brings another view and adds some detail to our interview.

BORIS PLATEAU
Animator

Tarzan, Despicable Me, The Lorax, A Monster in Paris, Paddington

Q: Are there different types of Animators in feature film work?

A: Yes, there are several different types of animators and you might like to break them down like this:

Main character animators: (which I am) - Usually animate the hero's and featured characters.

Crowd animators - Animating all other characters and crowd characters.
For these you need a great sense of timing, good observation skills and a solid understanding of physics.

Technical animators include:
    - Character FX - Animating hair and clothes.
    - Visual effects - pyrotechnics, atmospheric simulations, particles, smoke, that type of thing.

Technical animators are required to have special experience with multiple dedicated software tools.

Q: Technology plays a major role in film making today, please tell me how it is changing the way you work?

A: Well, in my particular case, this is my life's work. I've been into animation software from the very start of my career so I didn't have to adapt from the traditional methods to computer animation. I would say that computer technology is the main tool that's used to build any type of film today be it animation of otherwise.

Q: With whom do you work most closely?

A: I work most closely with the director of the film. We get together very regularly and I show him/her our progress.

Here is the usual process:

The director will brief our team on a particular sequence and talk in detail about how they see the sequence unfolding. It is at these meeting that we have a chance to ask all of our questions and propose suggested solutions and ideas.

We will then disappear and create a rough mock up block animation as soon as possible to present to the director so we can continue to refine the sequence to the their liking. This process repeats until the director is plenty satisfied with our work.

Q: What would you consider the 'must have' skill set for a successful animator?

A: I'd say that the first thing is that you must love animation because it takes so much time and dedication!

- Then you need a very good sense of visual observation.
- Depending on the type of animation you need to become a master of your software and be able to make it sing!
- Practice, practice, and practice, and when you think you've practiced enough start over and practice some more.
- Exchange ideas with others and be open to all sorts of collaboration.
- Have the ability to listen to your mentors and not be threatened by people that are

trying to make you better.

- Never to be afraid of trying something new and different because our craft is ever evolving.

Q: How are Animators compensated?

A: In my case I receive a salary and bonuses when appropriate. I make a very good living but have worked diligently at my craft for many years to develop my skills to the highest level.

Q: Tell me something that most people don't know about you Boris?

A: Everything!!! No, seriously. The main thing most people would not know about me is that I attended the University for Computer Graphics *but* taught myself character animation. I learned animation at home!

Q: Do you have a favorite project?

A: Every project is an adventure and I've meet many wonderful people. Back in 2009 I was working on *Monster in Paris*. It was quite a low/mid budget movie, but the quality was good, and the team was amazing, not to mention the awesome emulation. Another one of my favorites was *Despicable Me 2*. We had an awesome team with extremely talented people.

JAKUB KROMPOLC

Rigger CG Production

IMDB - Captain America, Harry Potter, Tarzan, Total Recall, League of Gods

Q: Jakub, would you explain in simple terms exactly what a Rigger does?

A: A rigger is primarily responsible for building articulation systems for digital 3D models of a character, vehicle or a prop. He makes the controls for animators, so they can conveniently move the arms, hips, legs and so on. The second responsibility is called 'binding' where the rigger needs to apply constraints and deformers so the 3D model of a character appears properly in every pose the animator makes.

Q: How does being a Rigger on a feature film differ from a Rigger working on a computer game?

A: In most cases visual effects projects require realistic looking characters and other animated models. In film the density of the model geometry can be much higher as well as the complexity of deformation setup, which is often made of many layers of digital skeleton joints, muscles and geometry deformers for effects like wrinkles, bone sliding or skin fat jiggle!

Q: When are you brought in to design the rigging?

A: Yes, the lead rigger usually gets involved once the model geometry construction starts. Sometimes this is in the very early stages of a project where we want to test how certain proportions work for a character.

Q: How does having an art background help you in your job?

A: Art has always helped me look at my work in a different way than some might. When a rigger takes into consideration how the volume, the character`s muscles and how the skin moves, an aesthetic eye plays a very important role. Having the ability to be able to remove myself from the technical side and look at a character, as an artist is a great way of identifying problems.

Q: Is there a logical job progression to the position you hold? Could a modeler end up as a rigger?

A: Yes, I actually started as a generalist and would built my own models. Later, I found that I most enjoyed building rigs and so I started to focus on that particular skill set.

Q: There are various titles for a 'Rigger'. What is the difference between a Lead Rigger, Senior Rigger, etc.?

A: These titles are used for other disciplines across CG production and they denote different levels of capabilities and responsibility as well as the salary range. The range is pretty simple; Junior, Medium, Senior and Lead. Many times in the case of Lead Rigger, it's a temporary role rather then contract-based position. On a large team we might also have a 'Head of Department', which together with Lead position adds a level of management and sometimes takes part in hiring new artists; that type thing.

Q: What was the toughest film in terms of rigging complexity you've worked on?

A: One of my most challenging projects was setting up the mammoth harness for Roland Emmerich`s film *10,000 B.C.* This was in 2007 and I was still learning a lot about procedural rigging (using a computer script to generate rig) and the pitfalls of certain rigging so it was problematic.

Other character setups that have been quite challenging include:
- The battling oak trees for *Chronicles of Narnia: Prince Caspian* with lots of branches, which required a lot of research on my part.
- The Pegasus horse for *Clash of Titans* with a very anatomic muscle setup.

Q: How do Riggers get paid, and are there any residuals?

A: I can only speak for the UK but the range is somewhere around $35K to $120K per year. It's a very wide range because agreements are individual and confidential. A similar pay range applies to other disciplines as well, but riggers have the advantage of being smaller group. Most artists are generalists, modelers, animators or lighters.

The factors that play the most important role in the final contract settlement include:
- Years of experience
- Working for prestigious companies and on high profile projects
- Being positively recommended by people from within the industry
- Showing how you are an efficient problem solver and getting on well with others in the team

Q: I really enjoyed the film *White House Down*; could you use it as an example and tell us what you might be doing on a daily basis?

A: This project was not particularly heavy for characters, but we still had a lot of assets to rig. The first thing in the morning I check my email for any urgent requests or meetings and then address the list of models that need to be rigged.

For example: There was Abrams tank from the U.S. Army that needed to be rigged. We make all of our rigs procedurally and I use Eclipse, which is our main scripting application for Python and tweak the code with new features I might want i.e.: the treads that run automatically on each side of the tank. Next, I'll install that code and test it in Maya, which will automatically build the tank rig from the latest model and place it into the scene.

The automatic build process would do various other tasks like applying deformers, etc. Next, I'll publish this scene to our database as another version of the rig. Finally, I would send email to remind CG team so that they can update their cached animation model and replace it with my new version of the tank model.

I might also view dailies, which is basically gathering a group of people like a production assistant, CG supervisor and artists into a small cinema inside the company premises. There we can check our work on a large screen projection screen system and receive feedback from the supervisor or voice comments on new changes and tweaks.

Q: What was the most fun you've ever had on a project?

A: I would say working on the film *John Carter* and with the rigging team at Double Negative. Although the project was demanding, the team was very relaxed and we had a good laugh quite often. When you have a great team of people to work with everyone tries to stay in a good mood, even while we need to stay razor focused.

Q: From my chair it doesn't look like rigging is going away any time soon?

A: I agree, because it is needed for both key frame animation as well as characters animated using motion capture and face capture. Rigging is an important blend between modeling, animation and rendering and a big part of the 3D pipeline.

As the tools get more powerful the demand for detail and complexity in characters reaches new heights each year and, as the basic packages of commercial software like 'Maya' are not up to the task, experienced rigging TD's will be in demand to develop new custom setup software modules and deformers.

Q: Tell me Jakub; what's next for you – is there anything you haven't done that you'd like to in the film industry?

A: My current goal is to help grow the visual effects and animation division of Prime Focus World and it's very exciting! Long term I was thinking about trying my hand at directing and of course the project would need to include visual effects and interesting characters.

Q: I know that rigging is one of the few film jobs that require an apprenticeship, have you ever had an intern, or mentored someone?

A: With regards to interns and mentoring, I've never had an intern, but I was a mentor at CG Coach, which was online coaching for 3D animation students in UK. I've also done a number of talks on different rigging topics in Prague at the *SPLASH* conference for computer graphics.

I actually learned most of this trade on my own from books like *Maya: Secrets of the Pros*, and from DVDs like *Creature Creation Toolkit, Integrating Creature Animation Rig within a Production Pipeline, Hyper-realistic Rigging* or *Creature Deformers* - all of these publications were released by Alias Wavefront and later Autodesk. Paul Thuriot, Erick Miller, Jason Schleifer, Andrea Maiolo as well as others have also shared many tutorials that helped me years ago.

MUSIC EDITOR

When was the last time you've seen a film without any music at all? There are a few, but by and large, music is a major part of every film production and can be broken down into three main areas.

The first is the film score, which is the music that is sometimes thematic, as in John Williams's score for *Star Wars*. Then there is 'source music' like you might hear when actor Jeff Bridges walks into a bar and the band is playing. And then, increasingly, you hear pop music that is licensed from an artist or music label.

Before any of the final music is created, recorded, or licensed for a film, there is what we call the 'Temp Score'. This is the music that is painstakingly edited into the film typically for the purpose of presentation. The producers want to see rough cuts, the marketing department wants to show the film to focus groups, and the director wants to see their production with music to decide if the tone and feel is right.

I should also mention the importance of the music supervisor. They are well covered in my book *The Best Jobs in the Music Industry* so to keep from being redundant I've chosen to leave them out here. Music Supervisors are typically responsible for locating and negotiating licensing of the popular music you might hear in a production.

Music Editor Craig Pettigrew and I have a mutual love of cycling as well as music in general. He also understands the 'life balance' of hard work, family and 'me time' required for being successful and maintaining longevity in this crazy entertainment business

CRAIG PETTIGREW

Music Editor

IMDB - True Blood, Ugly Betty, The Jungle Book, The Killing, Monk, Buddha Eyes

Q: Craig, would you tell us exactly what you do and are responsible for in the filmmaking process?

A: This depends on what part of the process I'm involved with. Sometimes I am called on to a show before a composer is even hired to create a temp score so the producers and studio can test the film, to see how it plays. When this happens I'm working with the director and editor, and they have some definite ideas about music.

It's then my job to not only facilitate those ideas, but to bring my own to the table and start cutting cues to see how they play. Often, some wonderful discoveries are made. And often, too, we find out exactly what does NOT work. This process continues as they cut and re-cut the film, and as they continue to test their cuts to an audience.

If I come on with the composer (and if I'm not also the temp music editor) my job is to help the composer get ready to write, and to be his or her liaison to the cutting (Edit) room, and possibly the director and producers.

Each film or tv show is different, but overall I feel it's my primary obligation to help give the composer as much time to write as possible. Post Production schedules are always tight so any misunderstanding can cost the composer valuable time. So I help with detailed spotting notes, whatever markers or prep files are needed to load into his or her writing program, and any creative input that will provide shortcuts, as well as being an honest and resourceful sounding board.

Once the composer starts to create demos, it is frequently my job to mix those demos and prepare Quicktimes (QT) for those who are scrutinizing the composer's work. Notes are usually given, rewrites are done, and the process continues until the demos are signed off on.

At this same time, I am frequently concurrently working with the music supervisor, cutting songs that are either playing as source material (car radio, party, etc.) or songs that are acting as score over montage sequences. If that's not enough I am also responsible for keeping everything up to date in terms of any new picture revisions and that happens all the time during this process. It used to be that "locked picture" was something you spotted music to; now, especially in film, that's almost a laughable notion. Tv is a little more rigid, as shows are frequently chasing airdates and need to 'lock' in order to make the mix schedule on time.

Then, there's 'Scoring". For tv, that typically means that the composer records a primarily synth score out of his or her studio, and then delivers stems to the music editor. (Stems are the separate elements of the cue, i.e. Strings, Percussion, Guitar, Piano, etc.)

On a higher budget film, I prepare cues to be recorded on a scoring stage, complete with QT's with desired streamers (lines across the video as a visual reference for bars/beats and hit points) any pre-recorded tracks, and a click track for the orchestra. Depending on how much underscore music has been spotted, scoring for a film can take place in a day or over the span of several weeks, depending on amount of music and schedules.

Next for both film and tv the music is mixed and the elements are split out and re-recorded into stems for the music editor, so that the music mixer on the dub stage can have control over them when changes are asked for (which happens all the time!)

Speaking of the final mix, the music editor, with all of his or her tracks, is there to represent the composer (and the music supervisor). Minds frequently change, and what was once applauded, as a perfect cue now needs some surgery or "rethinking." Which means the music editor must step in, and either argue in favor of the cue as written, or cut and present alternate cues based on the entirety of the score that was recorded.

It's the music editor's job to know how to quickly assemble, cut, and present those alternate ideas; time on the mix stage indeed does equal money, and the quicker and better the job is done, the happier those paying the bills will be.

After the film is mixed, a final cue sheet must be done. This cue sheet details what music was used in the film, for how long, who wrote it, who published it, and the affiliation (ASCAP. BMI, SESAC, etc.) of those entities. The cue sheet is then filed with those affiliations so that the writers and publishers of the music can be paid their royalties.

Q: How long do you typically spend on a project?

A: I spent a year on *Alien 3*, six weeks on *Air Force One* (it was a re-score) and somewhere in between on most films. I also just finished up four seasons of HBO's *True Blood*. We've done about 10 hours of television over a six-month period.

Q: Is the job of a music editor a lonely one?

A: No. I usually work with a few composers, all of whom I know well. When I'm on the mix stage, frequently it is with mixers that I've worked with many, many times before. When I'm not mixing, I work primarily out of my house. While that may seem like a lonely time, I enjoy the freedom of being able to vary my schedule as I see fit. I can have a social life outside of work while I'm officially working.

Q: Tell me something that most people don't know about your job?

A: That I create a lot of the underscore (music) based on the shows existing library of music. Even among the people I work with, they all assume the composer writes music for every cue for every show. After a show's playback, all the producers will thank the composer for writing such a great score, when in fact I created about 65-70% of it using the composer's music from earlier shows.

Q: Run me through a specific project and how the process might work?

A: On *True Blood*, and much of tv (and shortened film schedules) it goes like this:

1. View a rough cut of the film, before the music spotting session. This is where myself, the composer, producer(s) editor, and director (though not so much in tv) gather in a room, view the show, and talk about music; decide where it starts and stops, and the creative ideas that they'd like the composer to address. I write all of this down in detail.

2. Generate music spotting notes from that spotting session. These are done in a template, and include in an easily readable format with all of the information given at the spot.

3. Start to cut songs given to me from the music supervisor for source cues in the show. There will be many alts per cue so I'll cut them, make QT's for the Supervisor for approval and then pass them on to the producers.

4. On *True Blood*, much of the show is tracked, meaning I will create cues based on the music in the "True Blood" underscore library. There are seven seasons so lots of original music has been written.

The time frame from spot to mix is sometimes very short, and there can be as much as 40 minutes of music in an episode, all thematically based (meaning characters and situations have their own theme). So I'll tell the composer what cues I think I can track, and proceed to create those cues, make QT's for the composer, and wait to get notes on cues he wants modified. Meanwhile, the composer is writing the new cues.

5. Once the new cues are written, and the tracked cues approved, all of those QT's are uploaded for the producers to view.

Notes are given on the score, and choices are made on the source music. Score cues are then adjusted or rewritten per the notes, and I will put together the final Pro Tools session

207

for the mix stage, which includes score, source, songs, main title, logos, etc.

After the mix, I will generate the cue sheet, and the music supervisor will fill in all the song information and file the cue sheet with the production company.

Q: Do you work with the director and producer? Tell us about this interaction.

A: In tv, I only work with producers. In film, it's mostly directors.

In tv, the showrunner (someone who oversees the writing, editing, music, and final mix of the show – virtually all aspects) is someone I will be hearing from frequently, either directly or through the composer.

On a film, especially during the temp score process, I'll work very closely with the director, especially if it is a director I already have a relationship with. In both cases, I've had very rich and rewarding interactions; together, we can often improve on something that we weren't sure about initially.

Q: Did you have formal training to prepare for your job?

A: Not by design. I went to Eastman and Northwestern as a trumpet major, but actually have a degree from Northwestern in radio-tv-film. When I moved out to Los Angeles, it was to be a picture editor. I started as an assistant picture editor for documentaries for several years, until I happened into an apprentice music editor job at Fox in 1983. Eventually Segue Music hired me, and that's when my training really started.

Q: How are Music editors compensated?

A: We're a part of the Motion Picture editors Guild. We usually get paid by the week, at a rate that's at least the Guild minimum and if it's non-union work, we can get paid however we negotiate; by the week, by the episode, by the job. On *True Blood* it's by the episode, which is then divided into two paychecks. They also pay fringes, and health and welfare, making it a union show.

Q: Is it important to live in LA to pursue a career as a music editor?

A: Yes. There are some editors in NYC, and a few in London. But most of us live in LA, and will go abroad to score and/or to mix.

Q: What was the best time you've had on a film and why?

A: I just finished *True Blood* this past Friday, and that has been a wonderful four seasons of work (about 6 months out of every year). In the '90s, I did about 10 films with Mark Isham. Those were also fun, with my favorite being *Quiz Show* and *Fly Away Home*.

Q: What was the most challenging project you have ever faced and how did you solve it?

A: I was doing the temp on *Steel Magnolias*, the Herbert Ross film back in the late '80s. David Shire had been hired as the composer, so it seemed natural to try and use a lot of his music in the temp score. Very little of it worked, and big scenes (like the Sally Field driving in her car scene after Julia Roberts dies) just didn't fit.

Then I started listening to a lot of Georges Delerue and I found a perfect cue for that scene and his music just started falling in place and working all over the movie, it was just beautiful. After that they fired David Shire and hired Georges Delerue. I felt bad about it but I had solved a major problem that the filmmakers were having.

Every person I've spoke with has had a different experience and advice to share and unlike Craig who crosses back and forth between tv and film, Emily Swanson works primarily on film projects. It's interesting to me as a composer and musician to note the subtle difference in how they describe their jobs.

EMILY ROGERS SWANSON

Music Editor

IMDB - Mao's Last Dancer, The Way Back, A Few Less Men

Q: Emily, let's talk about your job as a music editor. What is a Music Editor?

A: Music editors are busy people and wear many hats depending on the need.

- I work closely with directors and editors to create temp scores.
- I create custom rehearsal materials for actors and dancers, coach actors through ADR   singing, and fix lip sync and dance sync.
- I sometimes provide playback on the set for dancers or on-screen musicians.
- I conform the composer's score to any picture changes.
- I source production music and edit songs to fit scenes so they start and end in the right places, have lyrics falling in appropriate places, and don't   interfere with dialog.
- I assist composers by programming clicks and streamers for orchestral - recording sessions, and by creating demos of their work.

- I create new cues out of pre-existing score material when the budget doesn't stretch to a full score or scenes are added after the score is recorded.
- I also provide spotting notes and cue sheets, and fulfill delivery requirements.

Some of what I do is creative (temp scores, editing songs to fit scenes) and some of it is technical (programming click tracks, on-set music playback). I prefer the creative parts but the technical bits are rewarding in their own way.

Q: Is reading music a requirement for a music editor?

A: I would say yes, although I expect many music editors try and get by without it. If you are editing songs to fit scenes or doing temp scores, then reading music may not be very important, but an understanding of song structure, and the concept of bars and beats, is.

If you work closely with a composer, you need to be able to speak their language. In an orchestral recording session for example, it's important to be able to look at the composer's score and understand what is happening. In classical music editing, it's essential, because the producer will notate which takes to edit together on the score.

Q: How did you train for your job?

A: I studied music (opera singing) and audio engineering at university. My courses covered music editing techniques, and my first job was doing music editing for a classical label. Then I went to London, thinking that would be a good place to get some experience in the audio industry; what I really wanted was to be a rock 'n' roll recording engineer. But the job I landed was with a little company of film music editors, and it was immediately obvious that I was in the right place.

I soon realized that my original career choice would have been a mistake. Audio engineers work painfully long hours in stressful (and dark!) environments, often with difficult people breathing down their necks, and low compensation. I am a classic introvert (someone who needs a lot of time alone to recharge) and it would not have suited me at all.

Q: Is Pro Tools your software of choice?

A: Pro Tools is the industry standard, although people who work with a lot of classical music sometimes prefer some of the other DAWs on the market.

Q: If I were a talented musician, with good audio editing skills and a great ear what might be a path that would lead me in the right direction?

A: I think it's important to learn the craft from someone with experience. So I would be getting in touch with established music editors and ask to shadow them, then work your way up.

Q: Are you paid as a sub contractor?

A: By the day, week or project. And occasionally by the hour!

Q: How does technology play into your job?

A: It is becoming very rare to work with live musicians. Helping composers prepare for orchestral recording sessions used to be the music editor's bread and butter, but it's not the case anymore.

Composers used to need a lot of help creating demos of their work to picture, but technology had made it lot easier for them, which translates into less work for me. Another way to look at this change is that now I get to focus on the creative part of my job and that's okay with me!

Q: How important is it to be in LA, or is it?

A: As I understand it, there are more music editors (and more jobs for them) in LA than the rest of the world combined. I believe LA has about 300 music editors. London supports about a dozen of them, and I think there are only a handful of them scattered around the rest of the world.

Q: Why do you think there aren't more women in the music/audio part of filmmaking?

A: I suppose it's for the same reason that there aren't more women in other technological fields; I think it comes down to the fact that we don't encourage girls to pursue interests in mathematics and the sciences.

Music editing is pretty far removed from playing an instrument. The path to music editing (or film sound in general) usually goes through audio engineering, though why that doesn't appeal to more women, I couldn't say. I did it because I thought it was a great balance of left and right brain activities; a beautiful blend of art and science.

I love working with music, but I didn't really want to be a performer; I liked the idea of applying my skills in a practical way.

Q: Tell me something that most people don't know about your job?

A: Music editors often have to walk a very fine diplomatic line. We are hired by the producer(s) to assist the composer and respond to the director's wishes, and sometimes those three parties can have very different agendas! Keeping them all happy can be a bit of a juggling act.

Even though I spend most of my time working alone on my computer, communication skills are really important. Directors are very visual people and sometimes need help articulating what it is that they want (or don't want) from a composer. Composers sometimes have fragile egos that need protecting. It's also my job to liaise with everyone on the music team (the sound mixer, the post production supervisor, the sound recordist, the choreographer, etc ... the list goes on!) and to make sure we are all on the same page.

Q: Anything else you would like to share?

A: There is skill involved in listening to a piece of music and knowing if it will work for a certain scene or not. I once asked a director what she thought of using a particular song in a particular scene. Her response was "I don't know, I'd have to see it." Despite being a creative and experienced film person, she just couldn't imagine it in the abstract, and most people can't. A music editor who can is a valuable asset to any production, saving a great deal of time. Time is money in this business…

I love my job! Any job can be stressful sometimes, but most days I can't believe I get paid to do this. Musicians are lucky that way; they are doing what they love.

COMPOSER

For those of you that have followed my exploits throughout the years, you know that I've had moderate success as a musician and composer. On the film side however, I have to be honest and tell you that of the four feature length films I've scored, you wouldn't be all that impressed. More than anything, it was great fun and a learning experience that gave me an appreciation for those that work hard and are talented enough to 'make it' as a film composer, like my close friend Greg Sims.

I've spent most of my music career either writing 4-minute songs, or living within the confines of a 30-second commercial score. I am blessed to have had a wonderfully rewarding time of it, both creatively and financially.

So, given my background and lackluster film composing attempts I am always happy to pick the brain of a successful film composer. Theodore Shapiro is an award-winning composer that brings a deep intimacy and structure to his work. He is part of a new breed of film composers that experiment as much with sound as tradition in his approach to scoring.

THEODORE SHAPIRO (with Ben Stiller)

Film Composer

IMDB - Walter Mitty, Blades of Glory, We're the Millers, The Intern, Spy, Ghostbuster

Q: Theodore, would you tell me a little bit about your role as a film composer?

A: In the course of a given project, I develop with the director an overarching concept for the musical score. I then compose the music to execute that concept, which helps the director tell the story.

In the case of *The Secret Life of Walter Mitty*, Ben Stiller directed and we discussed the idea of incorporating a voice into the score, and having that voice evoke Walter's inner voice; we talked about the idea of the music making a transition from evoking dreaminess to evoking presence.

I started by writing 'Walter's' theme, which gave definition to what the entire score would ultimately become. I worked on this particular score for close to a year, writing and re-writing the music as the picture was being edited.

Q: You have a longtime professional relationship with Ben Stiller. How did it start and what keeps the artistic energy and trust flowing between the two of you?

A: Ben and I started working together when he, as the producer of *Dodgeball*, asked me to compose the score. I had just worked on two of his films, *Along Came Polly* and *Starsky and Hutch*, and he liked what I'd done on those films. *Dodgeball* went very well and we've continued to collaborate ever since.

I love working with Ben. He pushes himself incredibly hard, and he pushes me hard as well; I have complete faith in his instincts. He never asks me to copy the temp score, or chase any musical fad. The impetus is always to do something really special and unique. That kind of trust really drives creativity in a good way.

I should also note that at the same time that he's pushing me, he's incredibly respectful and leaves room for me to push back, whether about the music or the film in general. On *Walter Mitty* in particular I think we had a deep and intense collaboration that was as satisfying creatively as I've ever experienced.

Q: Tell us about your education?

A: Going to The Juilliard School for a Master's Degree has proved to be very helpful. Juilliard gave me a number of compositional tools that I draw upon consciously or subconsciously every time I sit down to write. For example, the training I received in counterpoint from studying with David Diamond prepared me to incorporate fugues into my scores; studying privately with John Corigliano expanded my facility with writing aleatoric music; and so on.

My studies give me a lot of confidence when I'm standing in front of highly trained musicians conducting and recording a score.

Q: Do you have a 'typical' process when composing?

A: I'm a creature of habit. I work very intensely every day from around 9:30 to 5:30 and am generally stressed out at the beginning of a project until I nail down the tone and themes of the score. After that initial stress I'm ecstatic as I develop the score and expand that initial concept outward into more and more ideas.

The real challenge is to stay in that 'ecstatic' state as the initial rush of ideas gives way to the slog of the process - scenes are edited and re-edited over and over, the movie continues to evolve and change and you have to fight to keep perspective on whether the film that emerges from the editorial process is the same one you perceived when you started writing. It's always a question - 'Does my initial concept still work, still apply?'

Q: How do you get hired for a job; agent, referral, etc?

A: Sometimes it's based on some pre-existing relationship, whether with the director, producer, or studio and other times it's through my agent, or a personal referral. Once in a while it's just because a director has heard and liked something I've done.

Q: At the level you work, you are well compensated. Would you speak to long tail revenue and in particular what I call 'Mailbox Money' - performance royalties.

A: I'm not sure what to say. Four times a year a check shows up in the mailbox and it's wonderful and bizarre.

Q: What role does technology play in your job?

A: Technology plays a huge role in my work. I use a program called Digital Performer, creating very detailed mockups of the score. That way the director can hear pretty much exactly what the music will sound like in its final form. I also use a program called Ableton

Live, which is great for working with audio files. It's especially good at changing the pitch and tempo of audio files. That enables me to have recording sessions early in the process of writing in which I allow musicians to improvise, and then take that material and use it as flexible building blocks for the score. So for example on *Walter Mitty* this allowed me to do a recording session with José González and three other players early and use that material liberally throughout my score.

It's a great way to harness the creativity of great musicians and incorporate that into the compositional process.

ORCHESTRATOR

One of the most important but largely unrecognized team members in the world of film music is the orchestrator. This person works hand in hand with the film's composer helping to bring life to the film score. Often they are preparing the score to be performed and recorded by an orchestra and other times filling in spaces where the composer gives direction and creative freedom.

I've found that most orchestrators have an intimate understanding of the orchestra, including the politics, and musical sense of humor. (Which can seem somewhat twisted to outsiders)

Penka Kouneva is credited with orchestrating over 75 films, and is a great composer in her own right, having scored some 43 films. Penka was born and raised in Sofia, Bulgaria, started piano lessons at 6 and wrote incidental music for children's theater at the young age of 12.

In 1990, she ventured out of post-communist Bulgaria and came to the US to make a life for herself as a composer. She had only $130 in her pocket and a Duke University composition fellowship. In 1997, she made history at Duke by receiving the first-ever Doctorate in Composition from this distinguished institution.

Penka Kouneva has since been honored with the Aaron Copland Award, the Sundance Institute Composer Lab Fellowship and Meet the Composer Award.

PENKA KOUNEVA

Orchestrator

IMDB - Need for Speed, Ender's Game, Revenge, Kitchen Sink, Elysium, Gears of War, Vitrix

Q: Penka, would you tell us what you are responsible for, and maybe reference the *Ender's Game* film as an example?

A: Michael, it's an honor and a pleasure: An orchestrator's primary role or responsibility is to take a composers work (e.g., Cues, Sketches, MIDI files, audio stems) which can vary from very light to incredibly dense in their complexity and craft a complete score playable by a real live orchestra. We are truly the catalyst between the digital mock-up's and the real music that helps bring a film or game to life.

These days' composers need to produce mock-ups with virtual instruments to present their music for approval by the director, producers, and studio. Then they get too busy with revisions, or delivering audio assets so job of the orchestrator is essential - we are the support team for the composer.

Our job is to craft the scores, and plan the recording sessions. There are a lot of leadership and organizational tasks (related to the scoring session) that also fall on the shoulders of the

Lead Orchestrator.

Q: Tell us your team?

A: Besides myself usually acting as the lead orchestrator, I generally require the assistance of one or more of my fellow orchestrators that are of equal caliber and that I know I can rely on … especially since our postproduction deadlines can be very demanding and stressful at times.

When a very large project produces a massive amount of music, I will also bring on additional proofreaders to insure that we are not missing anything in all the minutia as we make our rounds getting the music ready for the scheduled recording sessions.

I also hold seminars before beginning of the job, to bring everyone up to speed and to explain all the parameters of the job once and for all. This way, everyone is on the same page. Things get extremely busy in the last week preceding the session and everyone is working 16-17 hour workdays.

Q: Did your long time professional relationship with Steve Jablonsky lead to the job of orchestrating *Ender's Game*?

A: Yes, of course. I began working with Steve Jablonsky in 2004 on a tv show called *The Contender*, then on *Texas Chainsaw Massacre 2* (2006), then on various genre films and games he was composing, then on *Transformers*. I was a part of a large team lead by Lead Orchestrator Bruce Fowler.

In 2009 Steve suggested that I co-compose the *Prince of Persia: Forgotten Sands* game and my team did the orchestrations. I am the one who assigns cues and then carefully proofreads the work of my team.

The most important part is to be integral to the music and to deliver what you say you can, for it is truly about quality relationships and of course performing at the level that is required in order to secure future work. *Elysium* and *9*, I got purely based on my reputation and past credits, without a previous working relationship. It was just the right fit, due to my work on the biggest sci-fi and fantasy franchises (I have worked on the *Matrix* 1, 2, and 3)

Q: What role did your formal education play in your career choice?

A: I was classically trained in Bulgaria, in the rigorous system for conductors, composers, and theorists. I've played piano since the age of 6, learned strings, and my mother, being a music theory professor took me to symphony concerts practically every week. I personally feel that formal knowledge and study is the key ingredient to success in virtually any field.

My passion for film scoring was ignited a bit later … around 1994. It was the combination of my passion for film, passion for collaborating with people, and naturally composing evocative, dramatic music - that made me choose the path of a film composer.

Q: Have you ever had an intern? What was the experience like?

A: I am known as the one who trains most people and opens doors to many young people in Hollywood, simply because I am always exceptionally busy, and also because I have a family and child.

The entertainment field always has the need and demand to work with interns. However, training them to get to the highest level is very hard and takes years of incredibly dedicated work.

My experience has been spending hours and hours, days, months in giving feedback, fixing their work to my exact standards, teaching them via feedback, assignments and score analysis and overall investing time, effort and passion into training my team. It's paying off, but it's been incredibly time consuming for me.

I've also hired a lot of women to work on my jobs. It is my desire to help pave the way for my fellow female composers and aid them in their own professional directions.

There certainly is no direct path to success in any creative profession in my opinion, so I believe in helping them learn about the potential pitfalls and giving them the necessary tools that they will need to be successful.

FOLEY ARTIST

Question time … who is responsible for creating all those footsteps you hear in the creepy scenes from *Into The Woods* or the heavy breathing in some passionate lovemaking scene? There's an art form that's been around since the day sound was added to film called 'Foley', named after Jack Foley.

In all the years since Jack walked 5000 miles on the Foley stage, the job hasn't changed very much, although the Foley Artists as they are called, are asked to create ever increasingly complex sound environments with a set of tools you might not expect to see in a recording studio: like a small swimming pool, four 10 different types of gravel!

Marko Costanzo is an energetic, over the top creative guy that has amassed a staggering 475+ credits as one of the top Foley Artists of all time. He was kind enough to take a break from his very busy schedule to talk to me a bit about his job.

MARKO COSTANZO

Foley Artist

IMDB - Into the Woods, The Giver, Foxcatcher, The Butler, Life of Pi, Shutter Island, Run All Night, and hundreds of blockbuster films

Q: Marko, would you tell us exactly what you do as a Foley Artist and maybe reference one of my favorite films, *True Grit*?

A: A foley artist creates sounds in sync with the actions you see taking place on-screen. These sounds are typically not recorded with the acoustical clarity required with today's sound mixes. During a film shoot the most important sound needed is the actor's dialog. It's much easier to re-create sounds on a Foley stage rather than to record them during the shoot with actors, directors and film crews present.

Many times the actions of actors take place on sound stages, which are typically made of wood, styrofoam and paint. This was very evident in a scene from *True Grit* when the young girl falls off a horse, tumbles backwards and lands at the bottom of a pit with snakes. In listening to the original sound track, I could hear the materials they used to construct the 35' deep pit. It was hollow and sounded like you were jumping in a wooden box. The 'set looked real enough, but it was far from being a real snake pit. With the help of my foley mixer George Lara, we re-created every sound you hear in that scene. The body tumbling down onto the boulders, the foot getting caught-up in the vines, the pebbles, rocks and dust rolling and settling down the pit slope are a few examples. We even did the snakes slithering on the ground, opening their mouths, tongues flapping and the snake biting the girl.

We record every separate action throughout the film in this manner paying close attention to every innuendo of movement, and make a sound in sync with every action on camera. The foley editors then shift these re-created sounds into place. Subsequently these sounds replace or embellish the original sound track.

Q: I believe that 'Artist' is a great descriptor for what you do. I was in the audio business myself for many years and amazed by the creative prowess of the Foley Artist Tell me about one of your most challenging projects?

A: As a foley artist, I find the most challenging jobs are animated films, because there is no production track. Usually the production track will give sound clues, which help in determining what something should sound like. With an animation, there is only picture available to assess how something should sound. So basically we need to start from scratch in order to record the proper sounds needed for a particular scene.

Life Of Pi" for example had both live action and animated sequences. Imagine a 30' metal lifeboat with a tarp covering half of the craft. The occupants on this craft include a young boy, a zebra, a hyena, an orangutan and a tiger. There were also 8 or so distinctive and different sound surfaces on the lifeboat that we needed to move these characters on to and off from. These surfaces included the wooden, the hollow metal bottom, as well as the wooden seats, the metal storage units beneath the seats, the canvas tarp, etc.

Directors like Martin Scorsese, Ang Lee and the Coen Brothers have always been very specific to us when it comes to the foley effects. Their vision of what something should sound like often times plays a role in the plot of their films and sometimes the director's notes are very specific

Here are a few examples of these notes:

- The pine needle forest should be soft and thick. The forest floor here has never been walked upon. - Joel Coen, *True Grit*
- Make the water trickle down his head and body like rivers flowing.
- Make the Hulk move through his environment, I want to hear the walls and furniture rubbing and deteriorating against his body. - Ang Lee, *The Hulk*
- The wooden box should be heavy, but also hesitant of being discovered. It does not want to come out of the hidden compartment in closet". -Thelma Schoonmaker - *Hugo*
- Make the Messenger stealthy, but keep him determined. We want to fool the audience as to who is approaching - *The Departed*
- Wallpaper peeling off walls should be thick, gooey, viscose liquids, like body fluids. - Barton Fink
- Wudang fighters avoid being hit. Make the fighting sounds without any impacts. I want to hear swishes and body rustles. - *Crouching Tiger, Hidden Dragon*

Q: Marko, you've worked on a staggering number of films. To what do you contribute your success?

A: To be successful as a foley artist you need to have a good sense of what things sound like in the reel world, (pun intended). You need to be willing to experiment with different props to generate believable sounds. As you move through a film you need to improvise a sound for every moment of the film, embellishing everything from a nose wipe to a punch in the throat.

In most instances you will not have the exact prop you see on camera. If someone on screen smashes a watermelon with a sledgehammer, I imagine I'd want to hear an explosive initial impact, with rind, pits and juice all colliding together in the air. I would want to hear the liquid "splish-splashing" in multiple directions. And of course this moving viscous mass must settle down onto a surface with the sound coming to an end in a "plop" or similar type sound. I can guarantee the sound you get from doing this actual action on a foley stage will be lack-luster and not at all what you imagine. The sound would happen too fast, and aside from making a mess, you'll need to repeat the action numerous times, using multiple melons.

You need to concentrate, exaggerate and figure out ways to give the impression you want to give, using whatever means necessary to achieve that perfect sound.

Most importantly you need to listen to your sound supervisor or who ever is calling the shots to make sure the sounds you are creating are the way "they" want to hear them. Foley is a subjective craft. What may sound, okay for a body hitting the floor in one scene probably won't work as well in another scene. You need to look at the actions, highlight the most obvious with sound and fill in the rest.

Q: How are people in your profession compensated? Would I be able to make a good living?

A: The foley artist is generally a freelance worker. Most foley sound stages will hire individuals as full time employees or on a per film basis. In Los Angeles, foley artists work in teams of two. You have a better chance of breaking in if you can get an experienced foley artist to bring you in as the second.

As you work on one film (and word gets out that you have done a good job), you will be invited back to work on the next project. The clients that are comfortable with your performance, will request you for their next project. Build up enough clients and you will make a decent living. Foley is performance. Doing it right, will get you hired again and again

Q: I would imagine that the best Foley Artists are trained or mentored. Have you ever had an intern, or mentored someone?

A: I have invited a number of interns over the years to come observe the process on the C5 Foley stage. Most were students looking to fill up their curriculum and some had never heard of foley before. I was one of those individuals that never heard of foley. I had thought movie sounds were recorded when the movie was shot.

Generally, if you want to pursue a career as a foley artist you need to understand that many of the clients we work for demand a quality of sound that surpasses anything you can edit out of a sound library. During my tenure at Sound One, a now defunct post production facility located in Manhattan, NY, I literally sat in silence for almost a year watching Elisha Birnbaum, the then number one Foley artist in NYC do his stuff. He was looking to retire, and that was a great opportunity for me.

Elisha knew I needed to get acclimated with what would be expected from his replacement, but he couldn't give up the reigns all that easily. The clients that were hiring Elisha, wanted only him, and considered me an incompetent. Then, suddenly his time became less available and I was ready to step in. After months of doing nothing in the studio, I was given some opportunities to show I was capable.

Q: Tell me about a typical day at work on the Foley stage for Marko Costanzo?

A: When working on a feature film, we work in reels. Usually a film has 5 to 7 reels with each reel being approximately 15 to 20 minutes long. Smaller budget films will allow up to 4 or 5 days of recording. The bigger budget films will use 15 to 25 days and more sometimes. We try to record all of the footsteps first and then we record all of the props.

A typical day on the foley stage would include making the footstep sounds for any number of characters. We will try to finish each character, using the same shoes on any surface the character walks onto. Once the footsteps are completed we will work on all other sounds. The props include everything from the body rustling of each individual character on-screen, to every other sound throughout the film. Face slaps, glass downs, body falls all constitute the prop list. We record sit downs onto chair, leather creaks for cars, the saddle movements for people on horses, etc.

It not unusual for us to use multiple tracks and layering to get the sounds we want to achieve. The budget of the film will determine how many sounds and tracks we use to record each individual foley effect.

Q: If I were interested in a career as a Foley artist what might be the best advice you could give me?

A: If you think you have what it takes to be a foley artist you should start practicing footsteps. I recommend watching people walk on the streets. Walk in step with anyone, then look at another person and walk in step.

Making great footsteps is more than half of the job requirement for a foley person. As you practice walking try to make a heel/toe sound with each foot. If someone is scuffing the feet on the pavement, you should scuff your feet on the pavement. Experiment with duplicating their mannerisms. Throw in a scuff or two on your own. Change the gait of your steps, or try walking with determination. You can try being casual with your footsteps or maybe walk like you are drunk. Remember that the person onscreen is acting, and you need to make the foley footsteps seem like they were recorded during the shoot. You need to know how an individual should sounds and to give character to your performance.

Alas the most important thing in becoming a foley artist is to get experience. Get a job at a postproduction facility that has a foley stage; be it a messenger or a clean up helper. Volunteer to search or obtain props that are not available. Being in the right place at the right time in invaluable. You may be asked to prove yourself at a moments notice. Be willing to just watch and listen to the sounds created. Listen to the feedback from the supervisor. Offer to be the sound editor / foley artist on a student film. Get a sound recorder and start banging stuff together.

Don't get discouraged. If you are given an opportunity to make some noise on a foley stage give it your best shot. If someone in authority determines it's not the way they want to hear that sound and request a re-recording with someone else, listen to how that person performs it, and try to emulate that action next time. Eventually, with practice, you'll develop the ear for foley, and gain the trust of your supervisor.

Q: What is the most enjoyable part of your job?

A: You get to see lots of films in their infancy as they develop into wonderful works of art. I never get tired of sound supervisors saying they love my work, which translates into they will use you again.

Working on films like *Life of Pi* and *Hugo* has brought a lot of attention to our foley abilities and C5 Sound Inc., the company I have been working with for almost 25 years. I was a part of the Academy Award Nominated/Winning team for these films.

Four years ago *Boardwalk Empire* came to our stage and we had been nominated for Emmy Awards three years straight. We won the Emmy Award for Sound Editing two of those three seasons. Now, Martin Scorsese's film, *The Wolf Of Wall Street* had plenty of foley effects recorded, and the film is an amazing work.

Q: You live in NYC, away from the LA film scene; how important is geographic location in your business?

A: NYC has a vibrant film community with a number of post production facilities all geared to handle the massive amount of information needed to complete the feature films and television programs being released these days. The world has gotten pretty small with the Internet making everything easy to transfer anywhere. More and more films are being shot and prepared in NYC, then mixed in LA or shot in LA and finished in NYC. Geographic location is much less important because of the ability to transfer the mix elements anywhere. NYC also allows a 30% tax credit on films shot and posted here.

Q: What should the world know about you, aside from Marko the Foley Artist?

A: Being a foley artist has been a great career. Throughout my high school and college years I was a performing magician, entertaining children and adults. Upon finishing college I thought I would pursue a career in "Show Biz". I now like to keep my hand in entertaining by sculpting balloon animals and performing magic shows for local charitable groups. I enjoy scuba diving, skiing, movies and live musical performance.

DIALOGUE EDITOR

In many, if not most films, the voice that you hear coming from an actor's mouth has been re-recorded in a studio after the film has wrapped up shooting. Finding the perfect location on set with no traffic, or plane noise filtering into a period piece can be next to impossible so much of the soundtrack needs to be created from scratch including the dialogue.

As the name implies, a dialogue editor is the person responsible for pulling it all together including organizing the production sound and matching an actor's re-recorded voice to his/her lips on-screen to fit perfectly, so that we can't tell, even when it's a close-up and their lips are 10 feet wide on a theater screen

Larry Kemp is probably the most celebrated Dialogue Editor in Hollywood with a credit list much too long to list here.

LARRY KEMP

Dialogue Editor

IMDB - Get Hard, We're the Millers, Captain America, This is Forty, and over 100 other films

Q: Larry, you are without a doubt the resident expert on Dialogue Editing. Would you explain in some detail what the Dialogue Editor does?

A: To explain what a dialogue editor does, it's important to know that feature film sound is comprised of three major sound categories: dialogue, music, and sound effects. Sound that's recorded when the film is being shot is called production sound.

It mainly contains dialogue but it also contains other sounds the microphone(s) happen to pick up on the set: ambience, useful sound effects (FX), as well as distracting sounds that we try to eliminate or lessen.

The dialogue editor cuts and arranges production sound on several tracks, as well as integrating new postproduction vocal recordings so it can be mixed in an intelligible, natural, and seamless way within a scene. Narrative films always depend on the aural illusion of continuity.

If shots were strung together without dialogue editing and mixing, the audience would be very distracted. The story content would be there, but different background sound levels, room reverberation differences, crew voices, thumps, pops, creaks, and bad production dialogue would be very disturbing from shot to shot. We would constantly be aware of the movie making process and have a less magical experience.

By editing dialogue, we fix these problems by preparing tracks so a re-recording mixer can match or segue dissimilar sound takes to make a smooth transition from one line to the next. We also cut and paste pieces of sound to eliminate unacceptable noises. If there are no good solutions by using alternate production sound, we replace sentences, words, and sometimes even single syllables with ADR (Automated Dialogue Replacement).

An ADR editor is a dialogue editor who fits newly recorded lines to actors lip movements. To do this we often need to cut up dialogue and move syllables backwards and forwards in time, lengthen them, shorten them, use multiple takes, and substitute a new word or two into a sentence originally recorded on the set. New dialogue content, called added dialogue, is often recorded for an actor when his or her face is "off camera" in the scene. We edit that too, placing and pitching the lines to sound natural.

Good ADR recording, editing, and mixing is essential for ADR to contribute to the dialogue.

Bad production sound is always more acceptable than bad ADR.

In the end, the dialogue re-recording mixer plays all our tracks together and adjusts the tonal quality, volume level, and reverberation (to name only a few), and re-records our edited dialogue. Music and fx are similarly re-recorded, and are finally mixed together for the finished sound track.

When we all do our jobs well, few are aware that all this stuff was done behind the scenes to create the illusion of continuity. Different genres of narrative, theatrical movies generally have varying dialogue-editing requirements.

Action films driven by dramatic visuals and sound fx, are usually much less labor intensive for the dialogue editor because they often have less dialogue and have lots scenes where sound Ffx can mask subtle differences in dialogue quality. Of course, a fair share of the dialogue needs to be replaced because of location noise.

In comedies and dramas, however, production dialogue problems are more likely to be exposed. Generally more editing is required.

Currently, I'm editing both dialogue and ADR on *Anchorman 2*, along with Joe Schiff and Tammy Fearing, the ADR supervisor. Using added ADR, different versions of the film have different jokes, and get tested at preview screenings every few weeks to hear which ones get the most laughs. I totally enjoy supervising ADR, having had that position on *The Pineapple Express, The Five Year Engagement*, and *We're the Millers*. Good comedies make my work very enjoyable. I like to laugh.

Q: What's the difference between an ADR Supervisor, and an ADR Mixer?

A: An ADR Supervisor is a Dialogue editor who decides, along with the director and picture editor, which lines need to be re-recorded, changed, or added at an ADR (recording) stage. ADR supervisors give feedback at the ADR recording session as to whether the line can be synchronized well into the actors' mouths and integrate with surrounding production

The ADR mixer works at an ADR recording stage and is responsible for getting good recordings through proper mike selection, placement, and other recording techniques. Great ADR mixers are alert, creative and have excellent communication skills. Their contribution to film dialogue cannot be overestimated.

Q: Do you work directly with talent?

A: Yes, as ADR supervisor, there's a lot of interaction. Most of this contact takes place at the ADR recording stage, but sometimes we'll meet to record elsewhere. After a take is recorded, the director, actor, ADR mixer, and I decide whether the line can match with the usable production dialogue that was recorded on the film set. I also give advice as to how to get better sync or pitch when I hear a problem.

Q: What would you consider the most important skills for a Dialogue editor?

A: Acute listening skills, a sense of timing, quick visual perception, good organization, work ethic, and the ability to stay focused on details are paramount to being successful in this job. Being a creative problem solver is also a big plus because what we do is fix things, and the solutions aren't always apparent.

Q: How are Dialogue Editors paid?

A: Dialogue editors (union ones, anyway) are paid by the week. I don't believe there's a standard for non-union editors.

Q: What's your take on the future of a Dialogue Editor as a career path?

A: It will be a difficult path if you only specialize in dialogue editing, but if you apply what you have learned to excellent sound effects editing, music editing and mixing skills, a very satisfying career will lie ahead.

RE-RECORDING MIXER

As a film enters the final stages of postproduction there are small groups of people that will mix the film for theatrical release (as well as all other media). This is a momentous task, and on major releases can easily take 6 months. The re-recording team is typically managed by a person with the title of Re-Recording Engineer who directly interfaces with the films director and associated producers.

In my last book I interviewed Michael Semanick and was intrigued with this job. This time around I talked to another world class Re-Recording Mixer, Craig Mann whom has mixed well over 100 films including such blockbusters as *The Bourne Ultimatum* and *Captain America.*

Photo courtesy of Rodrigo Ortiz

CRAIG MANN

Re-Recording Mixer

IMDB - Whiplash, Eye in the Sky, Insidious, and over 100 other feature films

Q: Craig, would you tell my readers what you do as a Re-Recording Mixer?

A: Technically we re-record the production sound (dialog), ADR, music and sound effects that get delivered to the mix stage in a balanced and coherent fashion that suit the film. Blending all of those things together gives you what you hear in the local movie theater.

'In simpler terms you mix the film much like an audio engineer might mix a band's song?'

A: Exactly! On a larger scale film like *Captain America*, we begin with a round of 'Pre-dubs' where we take the edited dialog or fx material and clean and or balance them, possibly combining like material into a more manageable size. Often that involves reducing the number of tracks; for example there might be 120 tracks of BGs (backgrounds) and we condense them to 64 tracks. The same happens for all categories, in varying sizes depending on the food group. Dialog, Foley, Sound FX, Group ADR.

The 'Final' mix begins when we have all of the pre-dubbed material ready. Those 'pre-dubs' are then further reduced and balanced down to 'mix stems', which are typically a dialog 6 track, music 6 track, an FX 6 track, a BG 6 track, a Foley 6 track. At the end of the final mix, the major decisions and shape of the film is complete.

The final step is called the 'Print master'. Those aforementioned five mix stems are combined down to one master 6 track, which is what you hear at the local multiplex theater.

This is generally the workflow that takes place on a large-scale film. By the end, you can see you've gone through several rounds of 'Re-Recording'.

Q: What's the environment like where you work … is it like a movie theater?

A: The best way to describe where we work is in a movie theatre that has a huge mixing console in the middle of the room. Typically you work with one other person. On larger shows, you might mix with two other people. Sometimes on smaller shows, you mix alone.

With three people mixing the work is broken up like....

    Mixer1- Dialog
    Mixer2- Music
    Mixer3- sound FX/Foley

Two-person configuration is usually -

    Mixer1- Dialog/Music
    Mixer2- FX/Foley

Q: At what point in the production do you go to work?

A: That depends. Often, I'll be contacted before shooting begins, just to read over the script, identify any areas of concern sound wise and formulate a plan with the director and production mixer as to how best to tackle any issues. Getting involved early on has many advantages including understanding the director's vision of the sound track sooner. You might also have a thought about how to execute a particular bit of the production when you'd like to have special coverage.

On the other side of the coin, having a show drop in my lap at the last minute is not uncommon either! In these cases I need to get on the same page quickly with the director, editor, and others to figure out what assets are what and how best to complete the show in a timely fashion.

Q: How long does it take to mix a film?

A: The length of the dub and final mix depends completely on the budget. A show like *Transformers* can mix for two months. Smaller budgeted shows we usually try and shoot for a 10-day mix.

Q: I see that you were an assistant for about 10 years before moving up to the first chair?

A: I think assisting on a stage or a Mix Tech, as they're now known, is one of the most overlooked jobs in postproduction. A mix tech has to manage all the sound and picture assets that come to the mixing stage.

They are first point of contact for the picture department coordinating the picture specs with sound editorial delivering cut units to the stage and with the music department. Ideally, when the mixer comes in the room on the first day of a mix, the mix tech already has a lot of the setup and asset management under control and the mixer can sit down and begin worrying about mixing, and not where this or that thing is. They are also the first line of trouble shooting when something is malfunctioning on the stage.

Once the film is complete, the assistant has to wrap the show, back-up, finish-up any delivery requirements and get all departments anything they might need to wrap up as well.

On top of all that, anticipating the needs of both mixers and clients on the stage often falls to the mix tech. Weather it be knowing another piece of gear will be required tomorrow for the mix or getting clients set with Wi-Fi access and lunch orders, the mix tech has a very pivotal role on the stage.

Q: Why did you decide to become a re-recording mixer as opposed to say a music/audio engineer, or scoring mixer?

A: I enjoy working with the director and other creatives to really shape the final sound of the film. The real magic happens on the mix stage when you begin to decide what works together, what's not working, is it better to only play music here, maybe better to drop all sound out there. That puzzle is something that I very much enjoy.

Q: Tell me something that most people don't know you or your job?

A: My job is 20% technical, 30% creative and 50% political. The actual knob twirling part of it isn't particularly difficult. The building relationships, trust, client confidence, good word of mouth and repeat business is the tricky part.

Q: What was the best time you've ever had working on a film?

A: Working with Michael Rapaport on his documentary *Beats Rhymes and Life - The Travels of a Tribe Called Quest* was one of the best times I've ever had mixing. First, I love Tribe. I listened to their music growing up. Their music still stands up today and I'm a fan. Second, Mike was very open to everyone's ideas creatively and I felt like the trust that he had in us allowed us to raise the bar of the film higher which I believe is apparent in the final product. A lot of very talented people were involved in that film in all departments and it was an amazing experience.

Q: Have you ever trained or mentored someone?

A: I've been fortunate to have fallen in with some very seasoned people along my way. Watching them, listening to their work and at times talking to them about different aspects of the gig has been very valuable. I also have had the chance recently to mentor a few people. It's a bit of an odd position to be in as I still feel, and am, on the younger side for this job, so imagining myself in that sort of position catches me from time to time.

Having 10 years of assisting under my belt, I'm very familiar with the frustrations of trying to move up in this business. I think if I can impart some knowledge or manner or experience on someone or even to be able to be there to say to the higher-ups; hey this person is fine, they can do it, I'd be happy knowing that I maybe made their transition a little easier.

Q: What is the most challenging part of your job?

A: Weighing creative expectations, versus commerce, versus my own expectations is probably the most difficult part of my job. The director wants it to sound like *Star Wars* and *Terminator* but it doesn't have that budget and I have to get it to a place where all parties, including myself are still happy with the final mix.

Q: Personality traits we might see in a successful Re-Recording Mixer … for example, the ability to work long hours in a dark space?

A: Definitely endurance, organization, thick skin, ready to make sacrifices, even keeled temperament, cooperation, team player, and self starter just to name just a few.

Q: For someone starting out how might they get their proverbial foot in the door!

A: Assisting is an excellent way to start off. You get an up close view of how it's done at full speed before you have to do it. Good old fashion harassment, weekly calls or emails asking about openings make you stand out when it comes time to find staff a position. Get out there and hustle your own work. Don't be afraid to fail and fail and fail.

Q: Where should I live if I want to be in your line of work?

A: Domestically, Los Angeles is still the place to be. New York is also big. New Orleans is a player at the moment. Also, London, Toronto, Vancouver, New Zealand are all pretty happening. I know a few people who edit remotely, but it's pretty rare. Mixing, not so much though.

Q: Financially rewarding?

A: Yes, I get paid daily when mixing, weekly when editing. If you're lucky enough to get a few clients together, have good word of mouth, and do a few films that break out, you can make a good living. That said, it can take years for all of that to come together. Be prepared for the long haul. It won't happen over night!

PUBLISHER

Without books and trade magazines (forget the internet for a moment) where would we be? Like you, I get my information from various sources and for many years depended on trade magazines focusing on my areas of interest, which include music, golf, science, technology, and *The Enquirer* (just kidding, however it's its a great read standing in line at the grocery store).

I should distinguish trade publishers from others that include web publishing, and book publishing because they are more specialized and their future is more uncertain.

I connected with Stephen Pizzello at 'American Cinematographer' magazine and after many years he remains both informed and passionate about his work and the industry; we should all be so lucky.

STEPHEN PIZZELLO

Editor-in-Chief and Publisher

IMDB - American Cinematographer

Q: What drew you to the media side of the film industry Stephen - your path?

A: I've always enjoyed reading and writing, going back to childhood, and I've been ravenously consuming various forms of media all my life. At family gatherings when I was a little kid, I would always circle the dinner table with a tape recorder and interview my relatives ("So, how are you enjoying the ravioli?"), so I guess my journalism career was preordained. To this day I cannot eat my breakfast without a newspaper in front of my nose, although at some point I'm sure I'll give up the print edition of the *L.A. Times* and just prop up my iPad in front of the cereal bowl. I've always loved movies, too, but I didn't get truly serious about film studies until I reached college.

Q: Did you have any specific education that contributed to your position of Editor-in-Chief and Publisher of *American Cinematographer?*

A: Yes - after enrolling at Boston University's College of Communications, I began taking journalism courses. I also worked for *The Muse*, the arts and entertainment section of the B.U. campus newspaper starting out as a movie reviewer and then serving as editor of the film section for two semesters. The classes I took at B.U. gave me a solid foundation in "Journalism 101," and the *Muse* work gave me the opportunity to hone my writing skills while learning all the responsibilities involved in managing a deadline-oriented publication.

I initially intended to major in journalism, but on the advice of a professor, who felt I was already very well grounded in the basics, I chose to major in broadcasting and film. Even back then, I preferred writing about movies to actually making them!

Q: Does your job keep you close to the film industry, which you obviously love?

A: Very close. As editor of *American Cinematographer* I'm constantly in touch with top filmmakers — mostly cinematographers, of course, but also directors and other key members of the crew.

Over the years I've done dozens of set visits to many noteworthy productions - a few of the more memorable were '*The Age of Innocence*' and '*The Departed*' (both directed by Martin Scorsese, one of my filmmaking idols, and shot by the great cinematographer Michael Ballhaus); '*Pulp Fiction*' (I was actually sitting on set, on a sofa just a few feet out of frame, as Samuel Jackson delivered his famous "Big Kahuna Burger" dialogue), *Bram Stoker's Dracula* (a great chance to hang out with another of my idols, Francis Ford Coppola, and his son, Roman); *Batman Forever* (where Jim Carrey regaled me with zany humor for an entire afternoon while sitting next to me in his '*Riddler* 'costume); Tim Burton's *Sleepy Hollow* (shot on elaborate sets in England by Emmanuel Lubezki, who recently won the Best Cinematography Oscar for *Gravity*); and *Titanic* (during which I literally had to secure James Cameron on a crane platform by hooking my fingers through his belt loop while we were hovering 100 feet above a water-tank set in Mexico). Suffice to say, I could write a book about it - maybe someday I will.

In the course of my daily duties I interact with filmmakers (or their reps) regularly, and I frequently attend advance screenings of their new movies or social events where I can pick their brains about cinema. It's a pretty great gig for someone who loves movies.

Q: If I were interested in a career in film media what types of jobs should I be considering?

A: It's tough to break in on the print journalism side anymore, because many of the publications I grew up reading (*Premiere, Movieline*, etc.) are no longer around in print form. Most people who might have pursued that path are now bloggers, either working for well-established sites like *The Huffington Post* or starting up their own movie-oriented sites

I know a number of entertainment-industry journalists who have been able to make a good living by creating popular sites (Jeff Wells of hollywood-elsewhere.com comes to mind), but they all tell me it's very hard work to get a successful and profitable site up and running Jobseekers with good communications skills can also pursue careers in broadcasting, or in public relations or marketing, but so far I've stayed on the print journalism side.

Q: How is technology changing your business?

A: Over the past decade, digital technology has truly taken over, both in publishing and moviemaking. Our magazine is now designed entirely with digital software, and I don't pick up the phone nearly as often as I used to — instead, I find myself sifting through at least 200 emails a day. The print version of *American Cinematographer* is supplemented with a digital edition and a website (www.theasc.com) that features podcasts, blogs and other content, so we have to manage that side of our business as well.

We also have a significant presence on Facebook, with over 250,000 followers, and Twitter; both of those sites have really expanded our reach and our audience. In fact, our publisher is now encouraging everyone on the editorial staff to "build our personal brands," so I'm sure we'll all have our own social-media feeds in the near future. This kind of online interaction puts us in constant contact with our readers, and their input is very valuable; we can find out what they want much more quickly and then tailor our content to give them the most bang for their subscription bucks.

Digital turnaround times usually mean that a publication must keep its editorial content extremely timely and current, but we've discovered that our print magazine is archived by cinematographers for permanent research. That's enabled us to remain a long-lead publication, but we supplement the magazine's content with more up-to-the-minute coverage on our website.

When digital video began replacing film as the primary capture medium in the movie business, longtime readers often asked me in a panic, "What will happen to the magazine if film goes away?" Happily, the industry's transition to digital production tools has actually been a boon for *American Cinematographer*, because there are many more companies creating those tools — and booking ad space in our pages. There used to be only a few key companies that made cameras used on professional or even indie-level productions, but that field has really expanded in recent years.

Q: Is a job in film media a viable career? Why or why not?

A: I think film media will always be a viable career option for anyone who is passionate and driven enough to pursue that path. There's a lot of competition for media jobs, but if you have the skill set and the determination, you'll eventually get there if you're willing to spend a few years toughing it out on the lower rungs on the ladder.

Film criticism is no longer as fertile a field, but movie studios still need to market and promote their product, so outlets that offer fans coverage of their favorite movies or tv shows will always be around. Landing a job really depends on picking a particular discipline, focusing on it, and gaining the experience and skills that the profession requires. It also helps to know what kind of coverage you want to do or are qualified to do; there's a big difference between writing for more general entertainment outlets and trade publications like ours, which require very specific kinds of knowledge.

We've occasionally hired writers who came to us from consumer-oriented publications, but many of them weren't well versed enough in the technical side of filmmaking to earn a regular spot on our freelance roster.

Q: What is the most challenging part of your job?

A: Managing deadlines, pitches and, occasionally, Hollywood egos is the most challenging. In order to cover cinematography properly, my fellow editors and I have to track down filmmakers all over the world, and we often need to work around their very busy production schedules in order to make an article happen. Over the past two decades, interest in the magazine has grown exponentially, and I'm now pitched on stories by movie studios, personal publicists, top filmmakers, their agents — really, anyone who follows cinematography or has ever thought about picking up a camera. Any day now I'm expecting to field pitches from someone's housekeeper or dog walker; that may sound like a joke, but I've even been pitched by cinematographers' wives and kids! Of course, everyone wants to be interviewed, and the big cinematographers and studios all want their projects to be the magazine's cover story, but there's a limit to the number of productions we can cover, and we only have 12 covers per year. So, like it or not, I have to find a way to say "no" to some very accomplished people (many of whom hold themselves in rather high regard). It's not always easy telling an Oscar-winning cinematographer his pet project won't be on next month's cover, but that comes with the territory.

I also have to keep everyone else on track with our deadlines - our freelance writers and especially our publicity contacts, because their priorities are often very different than ours. In the years I've been editor, it's become much more difficult prying approvals out of the major studios for any production-related "assets" - especially the stills and behind-the-scenes photos we run in our coverage. Nowadays, everyone involved in production seems to have approval privileges for artwork, and the follow-up required to obtain those materials can be extremely challenging, especially if you're not a naturally Zen-like person.

Q: I understand there's no 'typical day', but would you tell me about one of yours?

A: After being aggressively awakened by my wife and three kids at about 6:30 a.m. (that's now known as "sleeping in," if I'm lucky) I'll usually hit the gym to clear my head and mentally prioritize what I need to accomplish for the rest of the day. Once I'm back at the house, I do my first round of email; then I head off to the *AC* offices, where I begin tracking all of the articles we're preparing for that month's issue. This usually involves another round of emails and follow-up calls to writers, publicists, studio reps, and cinematographers

- basically anyone who's lagging behind with interviews or materials that we need. Once I've worked through those items on the to-do list, I'll spend some time planning future issues — mainly scouting out movies to cover, which usually involves seeking tips or scuttlebutt from various sources to find out which projects sound the most promising. When 1 p.m. rolls around, I usually have a lunch appointment with an industry contact — a cinematographer, a filmmaker, a publicist, one of our writers, or an executive from one of the production-related equipment or postproduction companies that work closely with directors of photography. In the afternoon, it's another round of email, quick meetings with the editorial staff to track their progress, and/or visits to sets or industry facilities when those are on the calendar.

On some days I can make it home for dinner at a reasonable hour, but more often I grab dinner on the run while heading to an advance press screening of a new movie we're thinking about covering. Other nights might require me to attend an industry function — a social event to meet filmmakers, or a more informational briefing at a production or post facility. During Academy Awards season, which now stretches from November to March, this probably involves free food, celebrity meet-and-greets and "mixology," so there are worse ways to spend an evening.

Q: Have you ever had and intern or mentored someone in the industry?

A: In the past we've had one or two interns at the magazine, and I always find that experience rewarding. I vividly remember what it was like to move to California from Massachusetts with no job and no real prospects, so I'm always willing to help someone who's starting out if they are hard workers and sincere in their ambitions. I think I'm fairly well qualified to offer advice on journalism and niche publishing, and I like to believe I can impart at least a little bit of wisdom about the fundamentals of good reporting.

As editor of *AC*, I've also tried to help connect talented young cinematographers with the renowned veterans I've gotten to know over the years. It's very, very satisfying to me when a student or up-and-comer I've helped goes on to become a big name in the industry. That's happened several times, although it's always due primarily to the individual's talents and hard work. I also enjoy covering promising cinematographers in the magazine, because they tell me that the articles draw a lot of attention to their work.

Q: What's the best part of working in the film industry for you personally?

A: I would say it's the chance to see interesting or extraordinary movies before they've ever been screened for a wider audience, to meet new talents before they achieve later renown, and to visit established filmmakers on the set. As a cineaste who thoroughly enjoys talking and socializing with other movie buffs and very creative people, I can honestly say that my job offers a steady diet of intellectual stimulation.

IT'S A 'WRAP'

So there you have it: armed with information and advice from some of the film industry's top talent, it's now time for you to venture out, grab the ring and land one of the *Best Jobs in the Film Industry*! If only it were that easy, right?

I do have few pointers that might help you get the ball rolling. If you know me, then you know I'm a big proponent of interning, and mentoring in our business. It's still the best way to learn, connect and break into the business.

People in the music and film industry like to work with nice, talented people - in that order. Connections can be next to impossible to make because the best crew are always busy; you need to be persistent while respectful of their time. Here are just a few steps that might help:

- Join my coaching or mentoring program. I take a very personal interest in my members; *www.themastermentors.com*

- If you haven't done so already, join LinkedIn and take the time to create a strong profile (focused on the position you are seeking). I will be releasing a short e-book on my site to tell you exactly how to connect with the right people on LinkedIn.

- If you are just starting out, connect with local film schools in your area and offer to help out (for free). You will not only learn, you'll be making valuable connections with the next generation of filmmakers.

Once again I'd like to thank all of the fine people that have taken their precious time to share experiences and insight about their jobs and the industry with you; the aspiring filmmaker.

Lastly, I'd like to thank *you* for taking the first step towards a bright career in the film industry. I'll be looking for your name in the credits!

Michael Redman

ABOUT THE AUTHOR

Michael Redman is a mentor, technologist, author, and composer living in San Francisco, Ca. and Orlando, Fla.

"It has been a profound honor to be blessed with meeting so many incredible people in my lifetime. Every person I've met along my journey has in some way inspired me to be a better father, husband, professional, or create better music."

"Helping talented young people to better understand the world today and how to take advantage of connections, and mentoring is my passion. The rewards are great, the efforts small…who could ask for more."

Made in the USA
Columbia, SC
17 February 2019